HOWGILLS AND ░░░░ ▔▔▔▔▔ALE

'How lovely flows the Lune
Since time untold;
By gorge and fell-side, farm and field and wood;
By shingle-bed, and boulders hewn
And smoothed and gentled by the water's flood.'

H A L Rice

Howgills and Dentdale

A David Leather

Smith
Settle

First published in 1993 by
Smith Settle Ltd
Ilkley Road
Otley
West Yorkshire
LS21 3JP

ISBN Paperback 1 85825 007 2

British Library Cataloguing-in-Publication Data:
A catalogue record is available for this book
from the British Library.

Designed, printed and bound by
SMITH SETTLE
Ilkley Road, Otley, West Yorkshire LS21 3JP

For Gordon, who enjoys the natural world

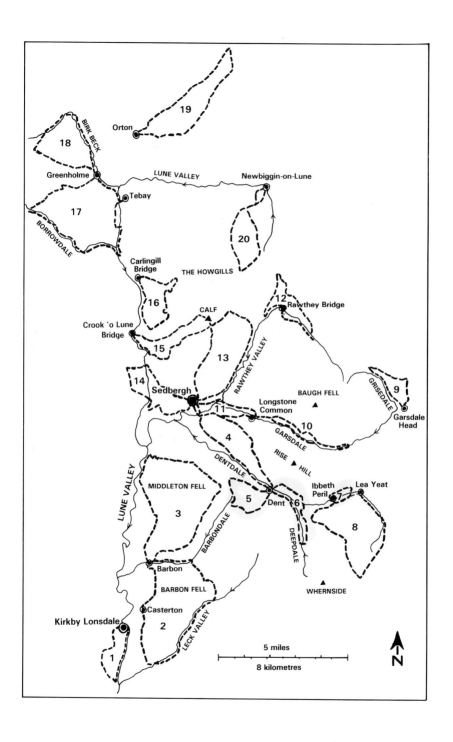

19

Orton

18

BIRK BECK

Greenholme

LUNE VALLEY

Newbiggin-on-Lune

Tebay

17

BORROWDALE

20

Carlingill
Bridge

THE HOWGILLS

16

12

Rawthey Bridge

CALF

Crook 'o Lune
Bridge

15

13

RAWTHEY VALLEY

BAUGH FELL

9

GRISEDALE

14

Sedbergh

11

Longstone
Common

10

GARSDALE

Garsdale
Head

4

DENTDALE

RISE ▲ HILL

LUNE VALLEY

MIDDLETON FELL

5

Dent

6

Ibbeth
Peril

7

Lea Yeat

3

BARBONDALE

DEEPDALE

8

Barbon

BARBON FELL

WHERNSIDE

Casterton

Kirkby Lonsdale

2

LECK VALLEY

1

5 miles

8 kilometres

N

CONTENTS

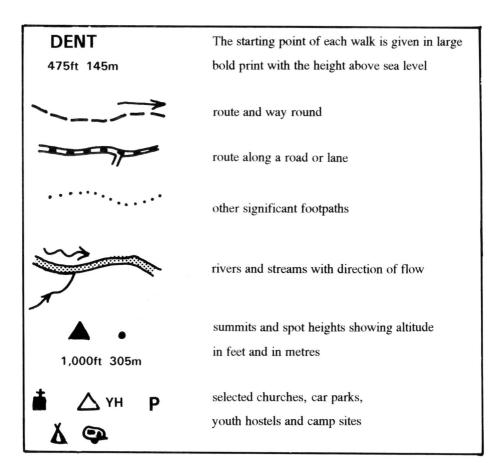

DENT

475ft 145m

The starting point of each walk is given in large bold print with the height above sea level

route and way round

route along a road or lane

other significant footpaths

rivers and streams with direction of flow

summits and spot heights showing altitude in feet and in metres

1,000ft 305m

YH   P

selected churches, car parks, youth hostels and camp sites

INTRODUCTION

The area covered by this guide is that drained by the River Lune and its tributaries, from Shap Fell to Kirkby Lonsdale. The many, branching dales are known as the western dales, from which rivers find their way to the Irish Sea – in contrast to the eastern dales which flow to the North Sea. The Howgills are the outstanding mountain mass central to the area and all the rushing waterfalls and becks, coming down from this triangular upland, eventually enter the Lune. Four of the twenty walks climb over these hills but the changing views of the attractive rounded summits act as a backdrop to many more. The Howgills are ideal for the fell walker. The smooth slopes, lack of walls and fences and few landmarks give the walker an unprecedented freedom. For company there are ponies, buzzards, sheep and curlews, but few people. It is easy to take the wrong direction on the Howgills and the use of a compass can be reassuring.

Middleton and Barbon fells border the Lune Valley further south and, to the east, the bulky shape of Baugh Fell – meaning 'rounded fell' – contrasts with the fascinating bare limestone of the northern scars of Orton and Asby.

Dentdale is the best-known of the western dales, but why not explore the valley of Leck Beck, Barbondale, Grisedale, Garsdale, the Rawthey Valley and Uldale? The beautiful Lune Valley, more poetically called Lunesdale or Lonsdale, starts in a broad vale north of the Howgills and turns south with twenty miles (32km) of unspoilt delights to Kirkby Lonsdale and beyond. Way to the north are the distant dales of Birk Beck and Wasdale, and, entering from the west, remote Bretherdale and Borrowdale.

Half the walks are within the Yorkshire Dales National Park, where there are useful footpath signs and waymarks, but many of the paths are little worn. Outside the Park, there is an excitement in route-finding without constant waymarks, or over-eroded paths. The area is crossed by the long-distance footpaths of the Dales Way and the Coast to Coast path, otherwise walkers are few and far between. Waymarking is improving and detailed descriptions of paths, which are kept to a minimum, may one day become superfluous.

The whole area is remote and wilder than some more popular walking districts. There are few villages or pubs and its is necessary to be self-contained with food and drink for the day, provision for bad weather, and plenty of time. You also have to be self-reliant with good maps and a compass – you may not meet anyone to ask the way! However, the people of the region are very friendly and will be only too glad to help.

The population is scattered, for the most part in isolated farms and hamlets, many of which are of great historical interest and some are points of local enterprises for tourists. Beyond the two towns of Sedbergh and Kirkby Lonsdale, there are only a few villages, though each is a delight to discover.

Sedbergh is the ideal centre for walkers, situated at the confluence of four lovely valleys, and in this respect is superior to any of the centres in the eastern dales.

Wednesday is market day, and Thursday early closing. There is a National Park visitor centre in the town and a good collection of shops and eating places.

This guidebook provides directions and clear maps for twenty of the finest walks in the district, ranging from three miles (5km) to thirteen miles (21km). It gives a background of historical events, explanations of the geology and scenery and the sort of wildlife and flora you might expect to find along the way.

The large maps are simple and easy to follow and should enable you to find your way round. Relevant Ordnance Survey maps are noted for each walk, but I recommend a new map which covers a large proportion of the walks: the 1:63,360 – one inch to one mile – Ordnance Survey Touring Map and Guide number 6, the Yorkshire Dales. For greater detail you cannot beat the 1:25,000 or 2½ inches to one mile (4cm to 1km) maps but you need five of these cover the area.

Thank you to Ted Gower who provided the beautiful line drawings and watercolours, to John Edenbrow for some of the colour photographs, to Jonathan Atkins for help with the flower chapter, Joyce Hartley for identifying plant specimens and Alan Meakin for imparting his knowledge of local birds. Thanks, too, to the four footpath officers that cover the area and to Sedbergh public library. An unqualified thank you goes to Midge for her encouragement and support on all the walks, in this and other books in the series. Special thanks to Mark Whitley and Smith Settle for their ever-available assistance and guidance in the preparation of the book.

When you are out in the Dales take back with you happy memories, notes, sketches or photographs but please leave undisturbed the wild flowers, rocks and fossils for the enjoyment of others. Respect the people who live and work in the countryside and remember the Country Code.

A D Leather
Ilkley, 1993

ACKNOWLEDGMENTS

Thanks are due to the following people for permission to reproduce the undermentioned illustrations:

Edward Gower: pp 12, 19, 20, 21, 26, 29, 39, 44, 52, 72, 76, 81, 86, 90, 99, 103, 105, 111, 115, 116, 119 and 125.

John Edenbrow: Front cover, pp 6, 15, 33, 36, 69, 91 and 95.

All maps and other illustrations were provided by the author.

PUBLIC TRANSPORT

The single rail link, via the Settle-Carlisle line, brushes the area high up on the Pennines above Dentdale and Garsdale. Dent station and Garsdale station are each suitable starting points for walks 8 and 9 respectively and train times from the south usually fit in to a day's excursion. But don't forget that Dent station is still five miles from Dent village. During the summer months a bus service connects with trains between Garsdale Head and Sedbergh.

Local buses are operated by Ribble, Cumberland and J Woof and tend to radiate from Sedbergh. The free guide *Dales Connections*, issued each year in April, is available from National Park information centres and provides up to date information about local services. (*Cumbrian Connections* is available from Cumbria County Council, Carlisle – 0228 812812.) Check timetables carefully.

Bus service operators:
Ribble Motor Services, Lancaster – 0524 64228.
Cumberland Motor Services, Kendal – 0539 733221.
J Woof, Sedbergh – 05396 20414.

Tourist Information Centres:
Sedbergh National Park Centre, 72 Main Street – 05396 20125.
Kirkby Lonsdale, 24 Main Street – 05242 71437.

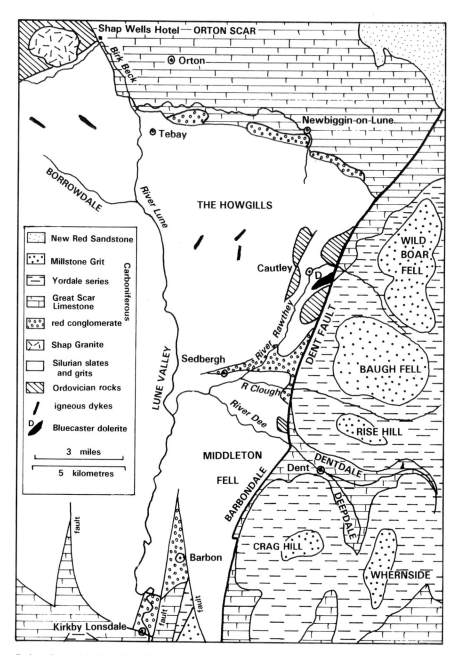

Geological map of the Howgills and Dentdale.

ROCKS AND THE LANDSCAPE

This delightful part of the country, lying between the Yorkshire Dales and the Lake District, takes some of its character from both, while retaining a distinctiveness of its own. The ancient rocks of the Howgills are an extension of those in south Lakeland, and the mild winters and early springs are a feature of this west side of the country, giving the westerly dales a more lush appearance. Unlike the Yorkshire rivers, the River Lune drains the west slopes of the uplands and flows into the Irish Sea. Many placenames – the -garths, -riggs, -scales and -thwaites – are similar to Lakeland names, and stem from the settlement and language of Norsemen in the tenth and eleventh centuries.

On the other hand a large part of the area is within the Yorkshire Dales National Park and was until 1974 within the West Riding of Yorkshire, although it is now in Cumbria. Dentdale and Garsdale, though narrower and shorter than the east-facing dales, still have typical Dales scenery. The town of Sedbergh looks in both directions, and tries to think of itself as Cumbrian.

The River Lune The Lune rises on the north-east corner of the Howgill Fells (*walk 20*) where it performs a curious change of direction. Starting on a short northerly journey as Greenside Beck and collecting several north-flowing becks off the Howgills, it turns sharply to the west at Newbiggin-on-Lune then, at Tebay, swings round another right angle to the south through the narrow Lune gorge, from where it continues to Kirkby Lonsdale, Lancaster and Glasson Dock to enter the Irish Sea on the southern margin of Morecambe Bay. Along its route, the Lune picks up several scattered tributaries many of which are secluded dales in their own right and of considerable interest.

The quiet valleys of Wasdale, Bretherdale and Borrowdale lie to the north-west of the Howgills in a little-known area on the fringe of the Lakeland Fells (*walks 17 and 18*). Wasdale Beck rises on the granite slopes of Shap Fell, becomes Birk Beck at Shap Wells and joins the Lune at Tebay, while Borrowdale Beck starts even further west, well within the Lake District National Park, and joins the Lune at the Roman fort at Low Borrowbridge (*walk 17*).

Further south, Sedbergh (*walks 4, 11, 14 and 15*) is the focus of three important tributary valleys, the Rawthey Valley, Garsdale and Dentdale. The Rawthey Valley – also known as Cautley – marks the eastern side of the Howgills after descending from the heights of Baugh Fell and the length of Uldale, where it is joined by Cautley Home Beck which drops steeply from the Calf in a series of cataracts. Garsdale's river is the Clough which begins in secluded Grisedale, encircles Baugh Fell on its southern side and joins the Rawthey a mile (1.5km) above Sedbergh. The River Dee of Dentdale flows through limestone country from the slopes of Whernside, picking up Deepdale Beck on the way and adding another dimension to the variety of scenery in the area. Barbondale partly follows the line of the Dent Fault and links Dentdale to the Lune Valley near Kirkby Lonsdale.

River capture The extraordinary pattern of the River Lune is the result of its superior power over other rivers and the capture of the headwaters of the River Eden. Before the Ice Age, the land surface stood at a higher level and rivers off the northern slopes of the Howgills flowed naturally to the north. However, a line of weakness west of Sedbergh (along ancient fault lines), together with the steeper slopes on the west side of the Howgills, helped to give more erosive power to the primeval Lune. It was able to cut back

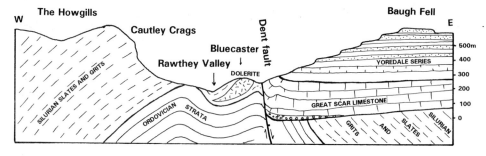

Geological section across the Dent Fault between the Howgills and Baugh Fell.

through a gap just south of Tebay – forming the impressive Lune gorge – and capture the north-flowing streams. Professor King in her *Geomorphology of Northern England* suggests that the breaching of the watershed took place within the Ice Age and that an early glacier aided the situation. Borrow Beck and Carlin Gill were the first to be diverted south. Exposure of the softer conglomerates near Tebay helped the Lune to erode its bed more rapidly in that area, which finally led to the capture of all the streams that flow off the northern Howgills.

The Howgills The whole of the upper Lune drainage is dominated by the Howgills, which form a compact and distinctive group of steep, dome-shaped hills, traced around by the Lune and the Rawthey. The poet Wordsworth, having passed by on a winter's day, referred to them as Sedbergh's 'naked heights'. The historian Whitaker wrote in 1823 of the 'piked points of Howgill' but the Ordnance Survey called them the Howgill Fells. For more than a century, travellers on

the railway have looked out from their carriage windows at these unique mountains, and the velvet-smooth hills now beckon enticingly to drivers and passengers on the M6 motorway. Yet many people pass by, and the Howgills, as most people call them, remain largely ignored and seldom visited by tourists. They are distinctive and noticeably different from either the Pennine or the Lakeland fells.

The oldest rocks These can all be lumped together and called Pre-Carboniferous. In the Cautley Spout area, and close to the Dent Fault, there are outcrops of dark shales of Upper Ordovician age (about 450 million years old) which contain fossil graptolites. These small dark imprints in the shales consist of slender stems with rows of angular 'teeth'. They are ancient colonial animals that lived floating at or near the surface of the sea; the fragile skeletons sank and were preserved in deep oceanic muds. Geologists find them extremely useful in dating rocks as they are fairly common and evolved rapidly. They

Steeply dipping strata alongside the River Clough, Garsdale, part of the Sedgwick Trail.

became extinct at the end of the Silurian period.

The bulk of the Howgills, as well as Middleton and Barbon Fell to the south, are of Silurian age (mostly between 430 to 415 million years old), the same as the strata across the southern part of the Lake District and some 60 million years older than the Carboniferous rocks of the Pennines. The Howgills are almost entirely composed of a very hard and compact sandstone – the Coniston grit. Being uniform and resistant to weathering, it has produced attractive rounded summits rather than rocky crags.

The Dent Fault The most important feature of the geology of the area is the Dent Fault, discovered and interpreted by Adam

Sedgwick himself, who first described it in 1838 as follows:

'I found that the [Dent Fault] passed along the south flank of Casterton Low Fell up Barbondale then across the valley of Dent, through the upper part of the valley of Sedbergh, and along the flank of Bowfell and Wildboar Fell; and that along the whole of this line there are enormous and complex dislocations'.

Along this major feature of the earth's crust, rocks on the Lake District side rose up some 8,000 feet (2,400m) against the horizontal strata on the Pennine side, pushing limestones into a vertical position close the fault plane (*walk 11*). The Dent Fault is a result of intense pressure and is termed a

3

reverse fault, whereas most faults are caused by tension in the crust and are referred to as normal faults – like those of Craven. The twenty mile (32km) long Dent Fault, roughly from Kirkby Stephen to Kirkby Lonsdale, is the best known example in the country of a reverse fault and forms a physical division between the two contrasting types of scenery – the smooth-flanked Howgills, and the horizontal limestone scars of the Dales.

Red conglomerate   This curious reddish rock can be seen near Shap, Tebay, Sedbergh and Kirkby Lonsdale. It consists of pebbles of Silurian age and occasional bits of weathered granite cemented together. It represents a land deposit which collected in hollows and wadis (valleys) in the desert landscape, and forms the base of the Carboniferous series of strata. The Pinsky beds, near Newbiggin-on-Lune (*walk 20*), lie just below the conglomerate and represent an incursion of the sea along a deep gulf. In the 1970s microfossils were used to date these as very early Carboniferous.

Carboniferous limestone   During Lower Carboniferous times, about 360 million years ago, the sea eventually covered all the land and thick layers of limestone accumulated. There are two distinct areas of limestone: the first is east of the Dent Fault and includes Dentdale, Garsdale and the east side of the Rawthey Valley. The second is a belt north of the Howgills between Ravenstonedale and Orton where the strata dips off the Howgills at about 10° to the north-east. Near Ravenstonedale is the most complete succession of Lower Carboniferous strata in this part of the country, and where, early this century, Professor Garwood first worked out subdivisions of the Great Scar limestone from the fossils it contained.

Dent marble   Above the Great Scar limestone are the alternating beds of the Yoredale series of rocks, limestones, sandstones and shales. These crop out horizontally along the valley sides of Garsdale and Dentdale, and on the sides of Baugh Fell. Dent marble comes from some of the Yoredale strata such as the Hardraw and Underset limestones. The limestones were got from small quarries in and around Dentdale, cut and polished, and sold as marble. Most of the quarries are now overgrown, but the three kinds of marble can be studied in Dent church. One is black with large fossil corals embedded in it, another is completely black, and a third is grey and contains large numbers of crinoid stems, fragments of the fossil 'sea lily'. Quarrying was all done by hand using wedges and levers, as explosives would crack the stone. Big blocks of stone were then cut by large saws, some by hand, but in Arten Gill saws and polishing operations were powered by water wheels.

Coal   A product of the past, coal occurs in a seam below the Main limestone near the top of the Yoredale strata. High up on Garsdale Common, some 1,750 feet (530m) above sea level, are dozens of old pits and shafts where, 200 years ago, large amounts of coal were produced for both limekilns and domestic fires. The former workings are scattered near the Galloway road, between Garsdale Head and Dent stations, where packhorses and carts were used to bring the coal down. Professor Adam Sedgwick remembered them when he was a boy in the 1790s:

'. . . the carts were of the rudest character, moving on wheels which did not revolve about their axle; but the wheels and their axle were so joined as to revolve together. . . . Horrible were the creakings and jykings which set the teeth on edge while the coal carts were dragged from the mountains to the houses of the dalesmen in the hamlets below.'

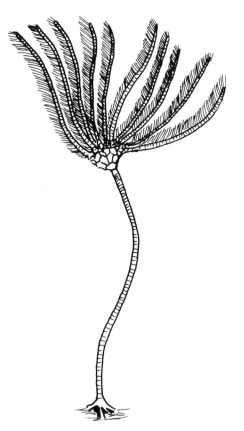

A crinoid or 'sea lily' was a very common animal in the warm sea of Carboniferous times. Fragments of the fossil stems crowd the Dent marble.

Shap granite   The famous pink granite from Shap, roughly circular in plan and over a mile (2km) across, is an igneous intrusion which cooled and solidified from a hot molten mass deep in the crust – perhaps five miles (10km) beneath the surface. The colour comes from the large pink crystals of feldspar, which makes it distinctive and easily recognisable. It is extremely durable, makes excellent building stone, and when polished has a great beauty of its own. Large blocks are used as decorative facing for banks and other important buildings, while small pieces are made into road chippings.

How the granite was dated is a classic. Slates of Upper Silurian age, in contact with it, have been baked by heat from the granite, which makes the granite *younger* than these rocks. Near Shap Wells Hotel is an early Carboniferous pebble bed containing eroded pieces of Shap granite, so the granite must be *older* than these rocks. Using only this field evidence, the age thus works out to be Devonian, the geological period between the Silurian and the Carboniferous. Dating by the use of radioactive isotopes has neatly confirmed this and put the granite at 393 million years old, or Mid-Devonian. In Devonian times, this area was part of a desert landscape (the Old Red Sandstone) where intense erosion occurred and no new sediments were deposited.

Igneous dykes, vertical sheets of intrusive rock, radiating from the Shap granite are of the same age and occur here and there, including two outcrops in Ecker Secker Beck at Cautley and a larger mass of dolerite on Bluecaster Side, between Cautley and Uldale.

Glaciation   Although the mountain mass of the Howgills was large enough to have its own ice cap during the Ice Age, ice from the Lake District and the Pennines may have hemmed in the Howgills ice, reducing the amount of erosion that could take place. The rounded summits of the Howgills, therefore, show very little glacial erosion. Cautley Crags are the only glacial feature, where the cliffs rise up behind the beginnings of a corrie, the higher valleys of Red Gill and Swere Gill being hanging valleys. A corrie is a depression that was gouged out by thick accumulations of glacier ice. The gouging effect was so strong

Cautley Crags from High Wardses, in the Rawthey Valley. The crags are the only feature of glacial erosion in the Howgills.

that tributary valleys were left 'hanging' high up on the sides of the deep glacial hollow.

The Lune gorge was deepened by ice moving from north to south, as suggested by a number of Shap granite erratics found there. The western dales had their own valley glaciers which were responsible for stripping off soil cover and revealing many of the scars which are so typical of Dales scenery. Combe

Scar above Dent also shows the beginnings of a small corrie with its own moraine of glacial debris.

Because the ice on the Howgills was hemmed in, and did not travel very far, eroded material was dumped close by. A thick mass of boulder clay can be seen in Carlin Gill (*walk 16*) where it has been eroded by the stream to form high cliffs of glacial till.

6

A syncline is a downfold of strata; this one, caused by a continental collision 400 million years ago, is above Black Force, with a view down Carlin Gill.

The valley bottoms surrounding the Howgills are also plastered with thick layers of boulder clay.

Some 10,000 years ago there was a climatic change and, as summers became warmer, the ice retreated. At first an Alpine vegetation took hold, soon to be followed by forests of birch, pine and alder. A wetter period fol-lowed when thick beds of peat formed on the uplands. Then, about 2,500 years ago, we entered a period with a similar climate to today's when mixed oak woods clothed the lowlands giving way, on higher ground, to birch and bilberry and heather communities. The scene was set for the influence of man on the landscape.

7

MAN AND THE LANDSCAPE

Prehistoric remains are few in the Howgill district, and the earliest monument is the fine stone circle near Orton which is made of rounded granite erratic boulders. A smaller one lies on the slopes of Barbon Fell near Casterton. There used to be one at Rawthey Bridge, but its stones were used to rebuild the road and bridge in the 1820s, when improvements were made for the coach service from Lancaster to Newcastle. Other late Bronze Age remains include one or two burial mounds to the north of Orton. From about the fourth century BC, Iron Age people lived in hut villages also north of Orton, and other traces occur on the side of the valley above Leck Beck (*walk 2*) near Cowan Bridge, and near Middleton and Hutton Roof. It is likely the higher parts of the western dales were only sparsely inhabited until the Norsemen arrived in the tenth century.

The Romans constructed the first ever road system in the country, and the Lune and Eden valleys made the best natural route from south to north. In AD 79, Agricola forged northwards from Ribchester to Carlisle and Hadrian's Wall, and the road passed through Overburrow, Casterton, Low Borrowbridge and Greenholme, all along the Lune Valley. Borwens, near Barbon (*walk 3*), is a Roman name, and there is a Roman milestone near Middleton with *MP LIII* (53 miles) inscribed on it. A branch road passed from Sedbergh up the Rawthey Valley, suggested by tell-tale names such as Bluecaster Side, Borwens and the Street. Two important military forts were constructed, one at Overburrow (*walk 1*), south of Kirkby Lonsdale, and the other at Low Borrowbridge in the Lune gorge (*walk 17*). For hundreds of years, the Lune/Eden

route became a highway for raids from the north, for wars, campaigns and rebellions.

Place names again hold the clue to the next incursion of people. This time of immigrants who came to stay and farm the land, mainly in the valley and lower parts of the tributary dales. Anglians, who arrived in the seventh

The Roman milestone near Middleton.

century from what is now northern Germany, left English name elements *ton*, a farmstead, and *-ing*, the 'place of so-and-so', which occur mainly in the Lune Valley: Whittington, Casterton, Middleton, Killington and Orton. Anglian estates were given to Earl Tostig, who from his manor at Halton ruled the Lune Valley as far north as Sedbergh. Two centuries later, the Danes settled to farm the lowlands, mainly of eastern England, though the placename *-by*, meaning homestead or village, is part of the name of Kirkby Lonsdale.

Norse settlement   There was a large influx of population into the dales around the Howgills when the Norsemen arrived in the tenth century. Howe is a Scandinavian word meaning hill, so Howgill means 'hill ravine', a name you could apply to the Howgills when you view them from the Lune gorge where the cleft of Carlin Gill is seen to cut deep into the upland mass. The Vikings, from the mountainous land of Norway, landed on the coast of Cumbria and Lancashire – via Northern Ireland and the Isle of Man – and felt at home in the empty hill country of the dales, where they could graze their sheep and cows and tend their pigs. The Norse were independent herdsmen who required large areas of grazing land and who had no wish to plough or sow. They hunted wild boar and deer, lived in longhouses and brought a language which became the basis of the Yorkshire dialect, leaving placenames such as *thwaite*, a clearing, *garth*, an enclosure, *holme*, an island, *scar*, a rocky outcrop, and *math*, a ford. Many of our words in everyday use have Scandinavian origins, such as: sky, window, egg, husband, thrive, ugly, happy, wrong and ill.

A glance at the map of Dentdale and Garsdale shows that nearly all of the dwellings are isolated farms, Dent being the only village. Each farm is built on the side of the dale, often by a side stream or spring, and

they tend to be evenly spaced out on both sides of the valley, with typical Norse names such as Swarthwaite, Hackergill, Dandra Garth, Birkrigg or Tofts. The distribution is in stark contrast to the Anglian settlement of Wharfedale, where all the farms are clustered into villages and isolated dwellings are rare.

The Normans   After the defeat of Harold in 1066, the Normans spread north and built many castles to maintain order and check incursions from Scotland. The early type of castle was made of timber, erected on a mound with an embankment and next to it a palisaded court. The remains are known as a motte and bailey and there are three in the Howgills area, each in a strategic position: Castlehaw Tower (Sedbergh), Castle Howe (Tebay) and Cockpit Hill in Kirkby Lonsdale. But none of these was replaced by a castle of stone, though the ones at Sedbergh and Tebay are in a good state of preservation and both may be visited (*walks 13 and 17*). The church at Killington is said to be on the site of another motte and bailey.

Soon after 1066 the Lune Valley belonged to William Rufus, and it was not long before the parish of Kirkby Lonsdale was presented to St Marys Abbey, York. The monastic east-west route from Furness to Fountains needed a safe crossing of the Lune and the magnificent stone bridge at Kirkby Lonsdale – later to be attributed to the devil – was built round about 1230. Erected on solid limestone, the two massive piers, supporting high graceful arches, have withstood 750 years of use by drovers, packhorse trains, waggons, pedestrians and even the motor car up to 1932. In a recess an old stone column bears the inscription 'Fear God, Honour the King 1633', and is sometimes referred to as the 'plague stone'.

The Normans also founded or rebuilt churches. The fine church at Kirkby Lonsdale has massive Norman columns with impressive patterning and large capitals, likely

9

to have been the work of craftsmen from Durham Cathedral. The eleventh century nave and splendid west door still stand in all their glory. The churches of Sedbergh and Dent, both dedicated to St Andrew, are also Norman with a few surviving original features.

Fortified houses There were constant threats of raids from the north: the Earl of Moray's men left devastation as they came down the Lune to join Robert the Bruce in Lancaster, and similar raids were repeated in the fourteenth century. This was the time of the building of fortified halls with defensive towers, and there are interesting survivals. Many a farmhouse was once a hall, and fragments of a tower or thick defensive wall are still to be seen. The end wall of the building was extended into a battlemented tower, often with a vaulted basement, known as a pele tower, as in the vicarage at Great Asby (*walk 19*). The courtyard was also defended by a thick wall and gatehouse – Middleton Hall near Sedbergh (*walk 3*) is almost in its original state.

When news came that the Scots were on their way, cattle were driven into the narrower dales and hiding places and, in the churches, weapons were kept in pike chests, ready for use. Like the farmers of the eastern dales, men of the Lune also fought at Flodden in 1513:

> 'Most lively lads in Lonsdale bred
> With weapons of unwieldy weight . . .'

Farmhouses Since isolated farmhouses are a strong feature of the Howgill district, it is not surprising that many are fine examples of period rural architecture. Early dwellings had thatched roofs with high pitched gables. A few of these can be seen incorporated in later buildings such as at Low House in Garsdale. From about 1650 there was much new building in stone, when stone flags replaced thatch. A porch was placed centrally, occasionally with a gabled upper storey, and a passage from front to back divided the house into two. The main fireplace had a stone arch, and often was built out on the gable end (corbelled), the extension of an internal hood, a place to smoke ham. Some of the old farmhouses have a third floor which was used for the spinning and weaving of local wool, and you can still see a few which still retain the large, cylindrical chimney stacks. The owners' initials and a date are often carved on the lintel above the front door.

In Garsdale are the old farmhouses of High Fawes (*walk 11*), Rackenthwaite and Swarthgill (*both seen on walk 10*). West Scale is a ruin in Garsdale with a turreted staircase (*walk 9*) and, in Dentdale, High Hall (*walk 4*) has two fine chimneys and Gibbs Hall is now a famous ruin. In the Rawthey Valley, Hollin Hall (1712) and Stone Hall (1695) (*both on walk 13*) are of particular interest, with Beckside and Low Haygarth in Cautley.

In the eighteenth century, wooden galleries, used for spinning and hand-weaving, were common on many of the houses. Today there are one or two survivors as in Railton Yard, Sedbergh, at Newbiggin-on-Lune (*walk 20*) and on Adamthwaite Farm in Wandale (*walk 12*). In describing the old galleries which jutted out over the narrow streets of Dent, Adam Sedgwick recalls:

> '. . . there might be heard the buzz of the spinning-wheel, and the hum and the songs of those who were carrying on their labours of the day; and the merry jests and greetings sent down to those who were passing through the streets.'

Great houses The broad valley of the Lune was an attractive place to build a mansion, and several important families took up residence in the valley. Just across the river from Kirkby Lonsdale is Kirfitt Hall,

The fine building of Stone Hall, with its rounded, Westmorland-style chimneys and three-storey porch, is one of the oldest in the district, dating back to 1595.

built in 1625 and, according to tradition, Henry VIII stayed in an earlier house on the site when courting Catherine Parr at Kendal Castle. Underley Hall was built in the 1820s by Alexander Nowell, a former Indian Army officer, replacing an older building. In 1840 it was sold to William Thompson, a London merchant, and in 1893 it went to Lord and Lady Cavendish-Bentinck, who became local benefactors. In 1979 it changed to an independent school for emotionally deprived boys. Barbon Manor was built as a Victorian retreat by the Kay-Shuttleworths, and across

the river are the halls of Rigmaden and Mansergh. Further north, the stately home of Ingmire Hall, where the Royalist Sir John Otway and descendants lived, was tragically destroyed by fire in 1928. Killington Hall has a ruined fifteenth century section, once the seat of the Pickerings. The newer part is dated 1640.

Famous people Dentdale and Garsdale produced several talented people. John Dawson (1734-1820) had an astonishing career. Born into a humble Quaker farming family at

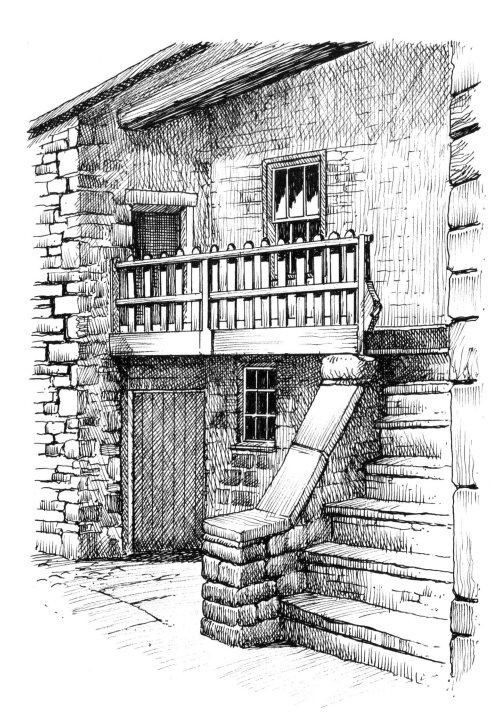

Raygill in Garsdale, John Dawson was an acknowledged mathematical genius. However, he devoted his life to helping the community as a surgeon in Sedbergh where, in his early days, he saved up £100 then walked to Edinburgh to attend lectures at the university. Stitching more of his savings into his waistcoat, he later travelled to London. But he settled in Sedbergh where his fame as a mathematician attracted, among others, several first-class honours graduates from Cambridge, known as Senior Wranglers. They would stay at the Kings Arms and pay Dawson five shillings a week for tuition. Three local men to come under Dawson's influence were John Haygarth, James Inman and Adam Sedgwick.

John Haygarth (1740-1827) from Swarth Gill (*walk 10*) in Garsdale became a notable physician of Bath. He was a pioneer of the treatment of infectious diseases such as smallpox by 'isolation, cleanliness and ventilation', which soon became standard practice.

James Inman (1777-1859), born at Fellgate farmhouse in Garsdale Foot, became principal of the Royal Naval College, Portsmouth, and the publication of his *Navigation and Nautical Astronomy* in 1821 led to the improvement in shipbuilding and changes in methods of navigation.

Adam Sedgwick (1785-1873) was one of the great pioneers of British geology. He grew up in Dent, attended Sedbergh School and became Woodwardian Professor at the University of Cambridge. Yet he often returned to his native dale and was proud of his origins. His *Memorial*, two volumes written late in his life, contain an amazing portrait of Dentdale, including boyhood memories of the 1790s

In Railton Yard, Sedbergh, is a rare survivor of the once-common wooden galleries used for spinning and weaving.

and descriptions of early Victorian Dent. He tells of the life and manners, work and worship of a Dales community at a time when the old ways were changing. (A reprint entitled *Adam Sedgwick's Dent* was published locally in 1984.) The memory of Adam Sedgwick is preserved by a block of granite, the well-known fountain in Dent's main street.

The household name of Mason's Ironstone China comes from Miles Mason, born at West House, Dentdale – now Whernside Manor. The colonial-style mansion of West House was built with the help of black slaves, brought back by the Sills from Jamaica where they had sugar plantations. Ill-treatment of the slaves became a local scandal.

Knitting industry The area became an important centre for wool and Dent, in particular, became famous for hand-knitting which developed in the seventeenth century with the making of good quality stockings and gloves. Large quantities of stockings were supplied to the army. A train of twenty packhorses went into Kendal each week from Sedbergh, Kirkby Lonsdale, Orton and Dent, and in 1801 it is recorded that 840 pairs of knitted stockings came from Sedbergh and Dent. Robert Southey wrote, in dialect, the story of Betty and Sally Yewdale, who were sent from the Lake District to Dent to learn to knit, and it is here he talks of the 'terrible knitters e' Dent'. Then in the eighteenth century, a coarse, oily yarn called bump was used to knit into jackets, long stockings, mittens and caps. Water-powered mills, such as those at Farfield, Hebblethwaite Hall, Arten Gill, Stone House and Rash, crudely carded and spun the yarn ready for the knitters.

Coalmining and quarrying On the high fells between the head of Dentdale and the head of Garsdale, surprisingly, there was once a thriving coalmining industry. From the seventeenth century until the 1870s it played an important part in the economy of Dentdale and Garsdale, supplying coal for winter hearths and fuel for the limekilns. Today there is little sign of the old pits over Cowgill Head or along the Coal Road.

Dent marble is not a true marble in the geological sense, but a natural limestone which takes a good polish and contains fossil corals or crinoid stems. In Artengill in upper Dentdale, marble quarrying started in 1770 and, by 1800, High Mill was converted from carding and spinning yarn to the cutting and polishing of marble, and Low Mill was a polishing mill from 1812 until 1907. The rock was quarried in slabs by the use of crowbars, and sawn by hand. Marble was exported all over the country and fireplaces were very fashionable. One of the finest examples of the polished rock is in the chancel of Dent Church. The eminent engineer W G Armstrong visited Dent Head for his honeymoon, was fascinated by the use made of the waterwheel and later used the same idea in one of his own works in Newcastle.

From about 1700, good-quality stone was quarried and dressed, which revolutionised building all over the district. At the same time flagstone slates were quarried near to the top of Baugh Fell, replacing thatch for roofing. Stone quarries on the south side of Garsdale and both sides of Dentdale were opened up.

The railways The main line over Shap – open to through traffic in 1848 – comes into the Lune Valley at Lowgill and proceeds through the scenic Lune gap to Tebay and Shap summit. Lowgill is where the now dismantled branch line to Ingleton joined the main line after passing over the arches of Lowgill viaduct (*near the start of walk 15*) and by the cottages of Railway Terrace. The main line crosses the sixty-eight foot (21m) high viaduct at Low Borrowbridge then, where the main line leaves the gorge, it runs along the

Lune Embankment. Here engineers built the railway on the former bed of the river, diverting it from its course. At Tebay the North Eastern Railway branched off to Kirkby Stephen and County Durham. For a distance of four miles (6.5km) from Tebay to Shap the main line climbs a steep incline of one in seventy-eight. The line passes over the Birkbeck viaduct (*walk 17*), Scout Green (*walk 18*) is at the half-way mark and Shap summit lies 916 feet (279m) above sea level.

The Settle-Carlisle line was opened to goods traffic in 1875, fifteen years after the first survey, and passenger trains were running a year later. The scenic line skirts the head of Garsdale and Dentdale as it leaps across gorges and dives into tunnels on its way from the valley of the Ribble, north to the Eden. The stations which serve Garsdale and Dent are high up and far from the villages themselves – Dent station is five miles (8km) from the village. Nevertheless, in the 1870s the railway brought modern transport to two isolated dales and an increase in trade. But the romantic 'Settle to Carlisle' is no ordinary line. It still generates a great following and is a reminder of some of the greatest achievements of the railway age.

Packhorse routes and enclosure roads
Craven Old Way is a packhorse route from Dent to Ingleton which climbs over the shoulder of Whernside (*walk 8*). One section is a thirty foot (9m) wide green lane, beyond which it follows a shelf of limestone before dropping down, to cross Force Gill and the railway. A second route to Ingleton follows Deepdale via a steep pass into Kingsdale. Adam Sedgwick described the introduction of small carts which slowly replaced pack-ponies and, writing in 1868, regretted that 'Dent has lost the picturesque effect of its trains of packhorses'. At the head of Garsdale and running from Garsdale station to Dent station is a minor road known as Galloway Gate which reaches an altitude of 1,760 feet

A farmer's first cut for silage in the Lune Valley, with Middleton Fell in the background.

(535m) on Windy Hill. It then curves round Great Knoutberry Hill and descends down Arten Gill. The road was in constant use for 200 years (until about 1870) for transporting coal from the pits scattered along it. It is uncertain whether the road was used as a drove road from Scotland or named by the use of Galloway ponies which carried the coal.

The enclosures of 1859 in Dentdale were one of the last in the Dales and the walled track of Occupation Road (*walk 5*) stands out to the south of Dent. It takes a high level route from the Barbondale road over to the head of Deepdale and into Kingsdale. It would have been used by the small quarries alongside it and may have followed an older packhorse way. From it are branches down Flintergill and Nun House Outrake.

Farming Over the centuries, farming has governed the changes in the landscape, giving it the appealing visual character it has today. The stone walls, layed hedges and farmhouses, the hay meadows, pastures and open moorland are all a product of a traditional way of life.

The richest, grade three land is in the lower Lune Valley below Sedbergh, and good meadow and pasture land (grade four) reaches far up all the branching dales, but the bulk of the area is upland fell, wild and

Limestone, burnt in limekilns like this one at Newbiggin, made lime to spread on the fields and improve the soil.

beautiful though limited in its usefulness. Most farms have a mix of permanent pasture and moorland.

The hay meadows are not only a source of winter feed but a botanical treasure, rich in wild flowers. Two dales which are environmentally sensitive areas (ESAs), where traditional methods of farming preserve the species-rich grassland, are Dentdale – up the dale from Dent – and Deepdale which branches off on the south side. Further areas are to be included in the future as the gradual move towards environmentally-friendly farming takes hold. Many farms rear beef cattle, but sheep farming is the most widespread. The Rough Fell sheep of the Howgills are attractive animals, with long, clean wool reaching down to the ground. However, such hillfarming is a finely-balanced business which attracts financial support, and any change in the future could alter the landscape considerably.

Cumbria The name Cumbria comes from the Welsh *Cymry* meaning 'compatriots' which referred to the Brigantes. The Kingdom of Cumbria existed until the Saxon king, Edmund, defeated the Cumbrian king,

Dunmail, in AD 945, somewhere north of Grasmere. In 1974, the name Cumbria was reinstated when the counties of Cumberland and Westmorland were brought together, plus part of Yorkshire and the Furness district of Lancashire. The boundary changes were a logical outcome of the geography and population distribution. That part of Cumbria which lies in the Yorkshire Dales National Park was in Yorkshire, and the rest of the Howgills and the Lune Valley was in Westmorland. The name Westmorland comes from Westmoringaland, as mentioned in the *Anglo-Saxon Chronicle*, and the Westmoringas were people who settled in the upper Eden Valley, so now that name is assigned to the history books.

Tourism The beautiful countryside, historic villages and the open spaces of the Howgills already attract discerning visitors. Part of the area – Garsdale, Dentdale and the southern part of the Howgills – are within the care of the Yorkshire Dales National Park with the information centre in Sedbergh. The northern part of the area is covered by the East Cumbria Countryside Project which has aims to protect the landscape, increase access to the visitor and conserve wildlife habitats. This body has been responsible for improving the bridleway between Sunbiggin and Great Asby (*walk 19*). Rights of way generally are being given more attention and it is to be hoped that soon many more footpaths will have simple markers.

Hard-working local people have set up many new businesses which are already a magnet to visitors. Dent, for example, has its own art gallery, brewery and designer knitwear (at Sophie's Wild Woollens). Nearby is Dent Crafts Centre (with restaurant) and higher up the dale beautiful handmade furniture at Little Oak. You can see rare breeds of animals at High Hall, dine at the many inns and eating places or see presentations by Spellbound Theatre.

on grassland, a good example of adapting to survive.

Some bird habitats:

By the middle of May, birdlife is at its busiest: the summer visitors have all arrived and the air is full of song as birds display, pair, mate and build their nests. The dawn chorus begins early, at the first hint of light, with the distant call of the curlew and very soon most other birds join in. Bird song continues throughout each day as each individual proclaims its territory and encourages its mate. By evening it is often the thrush and the robin that are the last to be heard.

Habitats include farmland with hedges and scattered trees, tree-lined rivers and streams, small patches of deciduous woodland, ravines and broad tracts of open moorland.

A most spectacular resident of the area is the buzzard, which is rare in the eastern dales, probably as a result of persecution. Peregrine, too, are doing well and a much smaller bird of prey, the little owl, is well-established in some of the valleys. A corn-crake in Dentdale was heard calling during June 1990. This once-common bird likes to be well-hidden in long grass, but the sort of rough places it nests in are becoming rare. Black grouse appear to be fewer in numbers, possibly because of a decrease in woodland scrub on the moorland edge and the growth of young plantations into mature trees.

The housemartin is not so numerous as it used to be; this is attributed to drought in Africa, so that fewer birds can make the long distances across a wider Sahara. A bird that has increased in recent years is the oyster-catcher, which has taken to breeding not only on the pebble banks along the rivers but also

Uplands (*walks 2 to 5, 8, 13 and 15 to 20*) The wild fells of the Howgills, Baugh Fell, High Rise and those of Middleton and Barbon, account for a large proportion of the area covered by the walks. You only need make your way a little way up out of one of the western dales and watch the sky above to see buzzards and kestrels, ravens and crows. On a sunny day, the large and conspicuous common buzzard likes to wheel and soar, often with rigid broad wings and tips up-turned, spending much time in the air as it circles around the lonely hillsides. If you are near enough you will hear its plaintive mewing call. The buzzard measures twenty-two inches (55cm) from beak to tail, is brownish with paler patches under the wings, and has bright yellow feet and legs. When perched on a post it takes up a hunched attitude, but may just as likely be seen walking on the ground looking for worms or beetles. Small mammals make up the main part of its diet, especially young rabbits.

The raven is much the same size as the buzzard, being a bit longer overall, and occupies similar territory. Both exploit rising air currents so that they can soar with hardly a wingbeat. Once they find a thermal they make a slow circling climb but, in the spring, ravens can also be remarkable acrobats when, in a display flight, a pair may tumble, roll and nosedive, sometimes flying upside down for a short time. The deep throaty croak may be the first sign of its presence.

The carrion crow, or dorp as it is called locally, is present in large numbers. This is an opportunist which survives in a variety of habitats, causing more damage to other birds and their eggs than all the other birds of prey.

They have even learnt how to fish for small trout in rivers which have partially dried up in recent hot summers.

Besides congregating over the rooftops of Sedbergh, swifts also frequent the highest summits where they spend all their time on the wing. They trawl the air, catching hundreds of small flies and spiders in their large gaping mouths, take short naps and even mate on the wing. Once they have fledged they do not set foot on the ground for two years. Swifts are the last of the summer migrants to arrive, about mid-May, and the first to go in mid-August. Two common birds, the meadow pipit and the skylark, both inhabit the fells from the lower slopes to the highest tops, and both have attractive song-flights. The skylark is slightly bigger, has a longer tail and a hint of a crest. Large flocks of starlings often congregate on the moors where they feed avidly on leather jackets, the larvae of daddy longlegs.

Each winter, flocks of snowbuntings are present on the uplands where they feed on seeds of sedges and grasses, which often stand proud of lying snow.

Cliffs and ravines (walks 5, 13 and 16)
There is no rival for the powerful peregrine, which likes high rocky cliffs for nesting. Suitable ledges are few and far between, but the open moorland is ideal territory for this falcon to hunt where it can see everything, using speed only in its famous 'stooping' dive. Near rock outcrops, the timid ring ouzel or mountain blackbird stakes out its territory with a far-carrying song of three or four shrill piping notes, and along the upper reaches of the becks the grey wagtail is numerous, its voice being a high metallic *tzitzi*. This is a bird of rocky streams where there is fast-flowing water; they feed on insects – often hovering for flies – as well as worms and small aquatic invertebrates. The dipper also likes quick-moving water: you may see its plump form perched on a stone as it bobs up and down before plunging into the water or whirring along, low and fast, to another perch.

Fields and pastures A successful bird, the lapwing is often seen in large numbers, feeding in the fields south of Kirkby Lonsdale, for example. In Dentdale and the narrower dales, it nests less frequently now, possibly due to the early timing of silage and hay crops. By midsummer, starlings congregate in large flocks – almost exclusively brown young birds – and have an efficient method of rapacious feeding.

From autumn through to spring, three members of the thrush family – the fieldfare, mistle thrush and redwing – are often seen together feeding on berried bushes. But they also take insects and worms when available, especially in the New Year when most of the berries have gone.

A welcome summer visitor, the swallow frequents farms and barns, where it finds a nesting place and a plentiful supply of flying insects to feed its young. Pied wagtails occupy a similar habitat and like to nest in stone walls, rocky banks or ruined buildings.

Look for the sparrowhawk, which is now quite common, as it darts low over and along the hedgerows and riverbanks. It takes birds only by surprise and speed.

Farmland in the Lune Valley and in Garsdale are good places to look out for the little owl. This small bird of prey, only nine inches (23cm) long, is active during the day and does most of its hunting at dawn and dusk. Its food consists mainly of small mammals, though they feed their young on worms and insects. Look out for it on a favourite perch such as a fence post, a barn roof or tree branch. On the lower slopes of the Howgills you may hear the 'little-bit-of-bread-and-no-cheese' call of the resident yellowhammer. The male has a striking lemon-yellow head, and both sexes have yellow underparts, a chestnut rump and white outer tail feathers.

They rarely travel far from their territory, but like some scrub for cover and a tree or two on which to perch.

Riverside (walks 1 to 4, 10, 11, 12 and 15) Sandy banks along rivers provide nest sites for sandmartins, as on the Lune below Devil's Bridge and the Rawthey below Sedbergh, where they skim and dive over the pools and shallows. The common sandpiper is another summer visitor which patrols similar stretches of river, where it nests in a hollow on the bank under a tussock or tree root, returning to the same site each year. The long-legged redshank frequents the Lune below Kirkby Lonsdale, while along some of the smaller streams and becks, dipper, grey wagtail and heron are common. It is always a surprise to see the graceful heron rise from the tiniest of side streams where it knows there is still some good fishing. Goosander likes a wooded river,

Sandmartins make their nests at the end of tunnels burrowed into sandy riverbanks.

The skylark always nests on the ground. Although mainly a vegetarian, it will also take worms and insects.

while the oystercatcher prefers a more open situation where it can feed in nearby fields, feeding on worms and slugs, far from the shellfish of its natural habitat. The kingfisher is rarely seen in the smaller dales but breeds lower down the Dee, the Rawthey and the Lune.

Lakes Neither of the two stretches of water, Killington Lake and Sunbiggin Tarn, are close to any of the walks, though both are notable for the birds they attract and are worth a visit. At Sunbiggin Tarn, north of the Howgills near Newbiggin-on-Lune, some eight thousand pairs of black-headed gulls breed, in spite of the many Coast-to-Coasters

who pass by. Coot and little grebe also breed there. At Killington Lake, on the M6 motor-way, Canada goose and tufted duck are both breeders, and great crested grebes and cor-morants are often seen.

Woodland Large deciduous woods are scarce, but broad-leaved trees often line the banks of rivers and streams and provide a similar habitat. In the spring and early sum-mer there is a variety of warblers and flycatchers. The willow warbler is wide-spread, but it is a delight to hear the blackcap and garden warbler. These two nest in wooded areas where there is enough cover, such as brambles, to nest in. They are closely

The wheatear is so named from the Anglo-Saxon hwit oers, *meaning 'white rump'.*

related and it is not easy to distinguish their song. That of the blackcap is more melodious and in shorter phrases, and it takes up a higher perch from which to sing. The blackcap is a greyer bird distinguished by its black or brown forehead and crown, but the garden warbler has no distinguishing features and birdwatchers refer to it as the ultimate 'little brown job'.

The wood warbler and willow warbler are leaf warblers, those of the leafy treetops, and have yellowish underparts and eyestripe. The wood warbler is more yellowish-green above and bright yellow below, and likes oak or beech woods with little undergrowth. The willow warbler is our most common summer

visitor and is less fussy in its choice of habitat. It is one of the first to arrive, and its warbling song of descending notes is a welcome sound of spring.

Both spotted and pied flycatchers are noticeable by their behaviour. Built to catch insects on the wing, they have large eyes, wings and tail. The way they dart from a perch for an insect is typical – although pied will feed on the ground, spotted won't! But the two have very different markings. The male pied flycatcher is, as its name suggests, black and white (the female being brown and white), but it is no good looking for spots on the the the adult spotted flycatcher, which is a dull brown and pale below. But look for the upright stance and the return to a perch after darting for a fly.

Two residents of the woodland are the treecreeper and nuthatch. These can be seen at any season, often easier in winter when there are no leaves on the trees. The nuthatch is an attractive woodland bird, streamlined in shape and bluish-grey above with a chestnut patch beneath. It never strays far from its birthplace. It nests in a hole in an old tree and has the unique habit of cementing up the entrance with mud until the hole is of the right size.

Siskins are present through the winter and may be seen on riverside alders. They visit peanut feeders in gardens and, in recent years, have occasionally remained to nest. Redpolls nest in fair numbers. They, too, like alders, as well as birches, but prefer stream-side willows for nest sites.

The redstart prefers to be on the edge of woodland. Its distinctive *weet* call is often heard before it is seen. Both male and female and the young of this elegant summer visitor have the distinctive chestnut-red tail. Gold-finches and greenfinches are seed-eaters, and you are likely to see them near to villages and farms. They are often seen feeding on thistle and knapweed. The goldfinch is well-named, with a broad band of yellow across its wings which, together with its red, white and black head, make it one of our most colourful birds.

Other wildlife:

Mammals The most appealing of the animals on the Howgills and Baugh Fell are the delightful semi-wild ponies which stand about in groups, quietly grazing. Even if they happen to be right in your path, they will ignore you. With long, flowing manes and tails, they vary in colour from almost black to brown, piebald and skewbald.

Foxes that roam the hills may travel miles in search of food, feeding on beetles, frogs and occasional rabbits or birds. In spring they

are a danger to sheep and lambs, and hunting helps control them.

Now they are protected, otters may be slowly returning to the Lune, but on a June evening in 1921, Thomas Bowness-Wright watched them from Rayne Bridge near Gaisgill:

'I peeped over the wall before I got there. What! The pool was agitated. . . He was making up under the bridge so I crossed the road and waited. Waves! He's coming! Two!! Two otters about 10lbs apiece. Sometimes slopping along under the overhanging bank, sometimes diving like two grey fish. . .' (from *Watcher by the Bridge*)

Otters are known to like the crayfish that thrive in northern rivers, and perhaps this food supply may help attract them back to the Dales. They also require 220 yards (200m) of undisturbed riverbank where there are plenty of tree roots and places to hide.

Stoats and weasels prey on mice and voles, and even rabbits and hares, all of which are common in the area but seldom seen. The stoat, which is of a paler brown colour, is the larger of the two with a black tip to its tail. A rabbit being hunted by a stoat becomes rooted to the spot with fear and makes no effort to escape.

Polecat ferrets, which derive from those kept for rabbiting, are quite numerous and can now be seen in the wild.

Roe deer are widespread in woodland, though not numerous or obvious to the casual walker. The only herd of red deer is a small one on Middleton Fell, though a deer farm near Sunbiggin Tarn is a good place to see them.

Butterflies If you see a small blue butterfly in April or May, especially if it is around a holly tree, it is likely to be the holly blue. A second brood has caterpillars that feed on ivy, and are to be seen in August. Between these times you may see the common blue. In the

A semi-wild pony on Longstone Common.

late spring both peacock and red admiral are on the wing. The peacock is a favourite because of its lovely colours. After a mild winter, peacocks are numerous when they come out of hibernation in the spring. The hairy black caterpillars feed on nettles, and a second brood is on the wing in August. The red admiral and painted lady migrate from the Continent each year and numbers can vary greatly. The summer brood of red admirals coincides with the peacocks, and both may be seen feeding on knapweed and thistles, together with small tortoiseshells.

Dragonflies Near to ponds you may see the common aeshna. The male has yellow and blue spots on the abdomen and the female has dull green spots instead of blue. Near to streams and becks in May, where the larvae breed, look out for the striking golden-ringed dragonfly with yellow rings round its long brown body.

Beetles The dor beetle is commonly seen on the Howgills, moving so slowly that it seems in danger of being trodden on. It is one of a group of dung beetles that help to tidy up the countryside.

Walkers have a distinct advantage in the observation of wildlife, and the regular walker will see changes from one month to the next or from season to season. Whether it is the first cuckoo in spring or the sight of a stoat crossing the road, it is worth making records of what you come across. A few notes can help build up a valuable picture, either over a geographical area or through the year. Local natural history and bird societies are always interested in sightings, not only to determine what is present but also to reveal changes with time.

FLORA

It is noticeable that the valleys and dales around the Howgills are more lush and green in appearance than the east-facing Yorkshire Dales. This is because of the westerly position, and the resulting milder winters and earlier springs experienced on this side of the Pennines. Although the rainfall amounts may be similar or even heavier, there tends to be more sunshine in the west – so the flora here have a distinct advantage. Soils on the fells are thin and lacking in nutrients, but there are rich pockets on the limestone, in sheltered ravines and on wet patches, where a variety of fascinating plants grow. At lower elevations there are occasional deciduous woods, hedgerows, ancient meadows and roadside verges, and the sheltered banks of rivers and streams, all of which harbour a wealth of flora.

In this brief review, some of the wild flowers are worth a special mention. In the spring, a small, rather insignificant flower may catch your attention – moschatel – which has a pretty little yellow-green flowerhead made up of four outward-facing flowers and one upward-facing one. The strict symmetry gives it the descriptive name of townhall clock (*walk 11*). Pink purslane is never common but crops up in unexpected places and seems to thrive very well on the banks of the River Clough in Garsdale (*walk 10*). This flower was introduced from North America and first recorded in 1838. It is native of Siberia too, as its Latin name *Montia sibirica* shows. And, of course, Grisedale is famous for its fields of marsh marigolds (*walk 9*). At Newbiggin-on-Lune the becks can be crowded with the lovely river crowfoot, white flowers with yellow centres, making a wonderful display in the early summer sunshine (*walk 20*). Wild

roses along the lanes of Dentdale (*walk 7*) are spectacular and standing out among the late flowers are the delicate pale blue spikes of giant bellflower, a sign of the coming to an end of another colourful season. The delicious milky blue is a special trait of this species in Northern England. In the south it is almost invariably a deep campanula blue (*walk 15*).

Rarities there are too. One of them is baldpenny or spignel, an unusual plant like a cream-coloured cow parsley but with feathery leaves. It grows near Howgill (*walk 15*), in one of only two 'ten kilometre squares' in the whole of England where it is found. An upland plant, not seen in the eastern dales, is the yellow mountain saxifrage which grows in nearby ravines, while on the Cautley side, the less common starry saxifrage is still to be found (*walk 13*). Cautley is also one of the few sites in England for the rare serrated winter-green.

The fells (walks 2 to 5, 8, 13, and 15 to 20) The rocks of the Howgills, and Middleton and Barbon fells to the south, are made up of Silurian grits and flags, and these, together with the heavy rainfall and steep slopes, have produced only thin infertile soils. Acid grassland is the resulting vegetation, where centuries of sheep grazing have just about eliminated species such as heather and bilberry, leaving mat grass interspersed with finer grasses of the fescue/bent type. Mat grass thrives especially on stable slopes, where it forms tussocks and bleaches to a pale straw colour from late summer. Sheep leave it alone as they find it too coarse and unpalatable. Flowering plants among the grasses include heath bedstraw, tormentil and heath milkwort.

The presence of a hill in the Howgill range called 'Knoutberry' suggests that, in earlier, sheep-less, days, when the hills were covered in bilberry and heather, the cloudberry was to be found there. No longer!

Springtime in the Howgills: a profusion of bluebells in Springs Wood near Cowan Bridge.

On most of the lower slopes, where soils are deeper, bracken takes over. This unloved plant spreads and grows by large cable-like roots and the strong fronds shade out the grasses. Patches of heather and bilberry survive on the shoulder of Middleton Fell (*walk 3*) where grazing has not been so intense. Cowberry grows there, too, a cousin of the bilberry but with red berries and evergreen leaves, notched at the tip. On the sides of Borrowdale (*walk 17*), among the tormentil and heath bedstraw, the blue form of mountain pansy is holding its own.

Baugh Fell has a cover of wet grassland where peat bogs occupy a wide area. Mat grass is dominant, but heath rush, cottongrass and mosses of the sphagnum and polytrichum groups grow well in the wet peaty soils. Heath rush is a wiry plant with a basal rosette of fibrous leaves which press close to the ground. The flower-stalk bears brown flowers or fruits. By late summer the leaves have a reddish look to them, and can easily be picked out among the mat grass. Flowering plants include lousewort, tormentil and sheep's sorrel and, in July, the yellow spikes of bog asphodel.

Cliffs and ravines (walks 5, 13 and 16)
Hidden in the shelter of ravines and out of the reach of sheep, there can exist a rich variety of plants. The west-facing Carlin Gill (*walk 16*) is a fine example. Here, on small patches of scree, certain plants are beginning to take a foothold. They include parsley fern, common in the Lake District but not often seen in the Yorkshire Dales. Alongside it, New Zealand willowherb has found a niche

25

Three species of orchid found in the area (from left to right): northern marsh, common spotted, and fragrant.

for itself and pearlwort, that weed of the garden lawn, makes up an unlikely trio.

On the cliffs and ledges, deeper in the ravine, grow two other attractive ferns, hard fern and maidenhair spleenwort. Deep yellow splashes are provided by the yellow mountain saxifrage, a fleshy-leaved plant that prefers damp places where it may be seen shining in the spray from a nearby waterfall. Other yellows are golden rod and St John's-wort, while common valerian, devilsbit scabious

and scurvygrass also add to the rock garden. A similar collection of plants finds shelter among the waterfalls of Cautley Spout (*walk 13*).

Limestone and limestone pavements (*walks 2, 8 and 19*) Limestone is confined to a belt north of the Howgills and another to the east which mainly outcrops in Garsdale and Dentdale. Soils on limestone tend to be more basic, giving rise to a good variety of flowers, including sweet-smelling herbs. Birdsfoot trefoil, wild thyme and limestone bedstraw are common, and occasionals, as near Masongill, include spring sandwort and small scabious. Just above Sunbiggin, near Orton (*walk 19*), carline thistle is surviving on the south-facing slopes. This is a plant of southern Britain and here only manages to produce fertile seed during warm summers. Global warming may allow it to grow even further north in years to come. Near Sunbiggin Tarn, large numbers of birdseye primrose lend a pink haze to the roadside verges; in among them are many orchids which include one of the finest displays of fragrant orchid, and colonies of the less common, but striking, flesh-coloured early marsh orchid.

Limestone pavements are a rare phenomenon worldwide. The limestone has to be pure, more or less horizontal and must have widely-spaced joints so that the grikes or clefts can develop (by water dissolving them out). A wide tract of limestone pavements on Orton and Great Asby Scars is now a National Nature Reserve (*walk 19*).

Within these pavements specialised species, including beautiful and rare ferns, survive in the shady and sheltered crevices. Wall rue grows near the tops of the grikes where there is most sunlight, while maidenhair spleenwort is found a little further down. In the deeper recesses, brittle bladder fern and the less common green spleenwort grow well. At the bottom of the grikes the larger harts tongue fern flourishes. This woodland plant survives grazing by growing in the deeper grikes. More tolerant of a dry habitat is the rarer limestone polypody fern, which likes a reasonable amount of light.

Growing among the ferns are woodland flowers such as herb robert, wood sorrel and dogs mercury. The rarer rue-leaved saxifrage also occurs, where it is in its true habitat. A careful search on the Orton Scar limestone pavements may reward the botanist with the two members of the lily family – lily of the valley and solomons seal.

Hay meadows (*walks 2, 3, 4, 6, 7, 11, 14, 15 and 19*) There are still many traditional hay meadows in Dentdale where, from about mid-May, sheep and cattle are cleared to allow grass to grow until it is cut for hay or silage in July and August. These are part of the Environmentally Sensitive Areas (or ESAs). Such meadows only receive light dressings of manure and contain a wide diversity of species. Among many others, wood cranesbill, pignut, betony and yellow rattle are typical flowers, and in damper pastures, bistort, cuckoo flower, meadowsweet and kingcups are common. The orchids, early purple and common spotted, as well as fragrant occur occasionally. Sometimes one species may dominate: there are examples in Dentdale of whole fields of bulbous buttercups, of pignut or bistort. This last plant was used traditionally for making Easter-ledge pudding, in which young nettle tops and barley were important ingredients.

An area north of Orton known as Orton Meadows is noted for a great variety of flowering plants. Soils are thick, damp and calcareous, resulting in some interesting and unusual species. In the early summer, common spotted orchid, birdseye primrose, globeflower and melancholy thistle grow well: later on, betony, saw-wort, devilsbit scabious and grass of Parnassus are to be found.

Wet patches (*walks 2 to 5, 14 to 18 and 20*) These vary considerably from one to another. Some are heavily grazed and only short-stemmed plants survive, while non-grazed patches contain a good proportion of tall flowers; some have acid soils while others may be described as basic flushes; altitude also has an effect on the species present.

Below Combe Scar in Dentdale (*walk 5*) is an upland damp hollow where there is an interesting collection of plants. The insect-eating butterwort and sundew both grow here, and other particular species are marsh valerian, lousewort, birdseye primrose and heath spotted orchid.

A similar collection appears at Shap Wells (*walk 18*). Birdseye primrose does well, both the ordinary lousewort and the taller marsh lousewort thrive, and ragged robin, butterwort, heath milkwort and heath-spotted orchid occur.

High on the fells, damp flushes often have water crowfoot, golden saxifrage, lesser spearwort and creeping water forget-me-not.

An area noted for its flora is on the lower slopes of Middleton Fell, between Fellside Farm and the road (*walk 3*). Betony, dyer's greenweed and meadow vetchling are common on drier places, while common spotted orchid, bog asphodel, marsh lousewort and marsh cinquefoil are outstanding in the marshy places, along with ragged robin, lesser spearwort and meadowsweet. Bog asphodel has a lovely yellow spike which flowers in July, and is as attractive as the orchids which are often found with it. A northern plant, marsh cinquefoil, has large deep-reddish flowers, of which the sepals add to the colour, and is related to the strawberry.

The riverside below Lowgill (*walk 15*) has creeping yellowcress, marsh woundwort, betony, melancholy thistle and imperforate St John's-wort. This last one has large golden-yellow flowers, the petals of which have small black dots.

Calcareous wet patches, or base-rich flushes as they are known, are associated with springs and water seepages along or below limestone outcrops. Beneath Gragareth, for example, in the Leck Beck area, lesser clubmoss, the pale forget-me-not and scurveygrass are to be found.

Woods and hedgerows (*walks 2, 3 and 17*) There are only small stretches of deciduous woodland and most of these are scattered along the lower part of the Lune

Valley. Those through which walks pass include Springs Wood on Leck Beck and Barbon Manor wood (*walk 2*), an unnamed wood by the Lune at Middleton (*walk 3* and woodland at Low Borrowbridge – also on the banks of the Lune – and the nearby Borrowdale Wood (*walk 17*). Other woodland occurs along rivers and becks as long narrow strips and still provide a habitat for woodland flowers and wildlife.

Springs Wood is an oak bluebell wood where wood sorrel, wild garlic and dogs mercury add to the carpet of bluebells. Although the bluebell has a small bulb, it reproduces mainly by its seeds, so the picking of bluebells has been discouraged and trampling of the leaves can kill them off altogether. The wood is noted for a variety of attractive ferns.

Just above Middleton Hall, along the river, there is a lovely deciduous wood where, besides bluebells, there are greater stitchwort, yellow pimpernel, hedge woundwort, red campion and water avens, all adding colour to the woodland floor. The wood at Low Borrowbridge is very similar, with enchanters nightshade, foxglove and giant bellflower. In springtime, here is a fine show of the elegant meadow saxifrage, spreading from the nearby field borders into the woodland fringe.

In the river valleys, hedgerows replace stone walls – but they are no ordinary hedges. This part of the country is noted for its 'layed' hedges. As young trees grow, they are partially cut through and brought into a horizontal position, and woven into a neat barrier, impenetrable to grazing animals.

The display of tree blossom in the Lune/ Dentdale area is outstanding where there is a succession of blossom for four of five months, followed by the equally attractive and colourful fruits which last until well into the winter, providing the bird population with a vital food supply.

Blackthorn is the first to come into flower in March when a froth of white covers the

Giant bellflower, and a detail of its flower.

leafless trees. These are followed by rowan which are very common in the hedgerows, then bird cherry and hawthorn take over for a few weeks before crab apple and wild roses decorate the country lanes. The blossom of the majestic wild cherry stands out in some hedgerows and small woodlands. By August the rowan berries are already turning a bright red and the hips, too, are large and shining in shades of red to purple. The haws add red

of a deeper hue, and blackthorn is decorated with sloes, still pristine in their silvery, waxy bloom. Damsons, wild cherries and crab apples add to the variety, and a strange sight are the 'woolly' skeins on the bird cherry hedges, caused by the bird cherry ermine moth.

Ferns and fungi (*most walks*) Ferns are a feature of the rocky gills, the limestone pavements as well as the small woodlands. Their fronds unfurl and carry spores on the undersides, and, with practice, it is easy to recognise many of them from their shape and habitat. Many of the old stone walls in the lanes carry a profusion of ferns. A lane near Whittington (*walk 1*) has the smooth fronds of harts tongue, the delicate maidenhair spleenwort with a shiny black stem, polypody, which has long fronds with equal lobes, and clumps of the irregular, leafy fronds of wall rue. Parsley fern grows on the screes around the Howgills (*walk 16*), and rigid buckler fern and limestone polypody are rarities of limestone pavements (*walk 19*).

From late summer it is well worth keeping an eye open for fungi, which often produce amazing, but short-lived, displays (*walk 2*). Fly agaric, red with white spots, is well-known and one of the most attractive. Stinkhorn is another obvious species from its putrid smell. The milkcaps are a group of gill fungi which range in colour from orange to dark brown, but if you break the cap, drops of a milky fluid ooze out, and this distinguishes them. Puffballs and field mushrooms grow in more open grassland (*walk 19*) and both can grow large. The edible mushroom makes the most delicious eating. Its gills are pink at first, turning brown, then almost black. Beware of the poisonous yellow-staining mushroom, which produces a yellow stain when rubbed, and the destroying angel which has white gills. A good book on fungi is an essential guide, though a friend with first-hand knowledge is even better.

29

WALK 1: RIVER WALK FROM KIRKBY LONSDALE

Start: Kirkby Lonsdale. Grid Ref: 611 787
Distance: 6½ miles (10½km)
OS Maps: Pathfinder 628 (mainly) and 627 or Landranger 97
Walking Time: 3½ hours

Explore the corners of the delightful little market town of Kirkby Lonsdale, and from its ancient and interesting church see Ruskin's View and follow two and a half miles (4km) of attractive riverside walk, south past Devil's Bridge along the Lune. Turn into the small village of Whittington, whose church stands in a picturesque position overlooking the river, then on to Sellet Hall, noted for its herb garden. The river is particularly good for birdwatchers and Kirkby Lonsdale holds a wealth of historical interest. There are three small car parks in Kirkby Lonsdale.

Situated on the edge of Cumbria near the border with Lancashire, amid fine river and fell scenery, Kirkby Lonsdale is a fascinating little town with a long history. Mentioned in *Domesday Book* of 1086, the name means 'church village in the Lune Valley'. The charter of 1227 was granted by Henry III and markets were held in Market Street, Horsemarket and Swinemarket. There is still a market every Thursday in the nineteenth century market square. The monument in the square is a mock-medieval butter cross erected early this century.

The many old inns and hotels are a mark of the importance of the town in days when packhorse trains, drovers and coaches stopped here. Many, such as the Sun, the Kings Arms, the Red Dragon and the Green Dragon, date back 400 years with old oak beams and staircases and, on Market Street, the Sun still retains its seventeenth century frontage.

John Ruskin was enraptured with the town:

'I do not know in all my country, still less in France or Italy, a place more naturally divine . . . than Kirkby Lonsdale.'

Modern Kirkby Lonsdale is a bustling and thriving market town, holding many attractions for visitors. A woollens shop in the market square is the outlet for the sheepskin factory at Cowan Bridge. There is a good second-hand bookshop, many other specialist shops, a tourist information centre and in September a Victorian fair is held.

Starting the walk at the market square, turn right along Main Street then right onto Mill Brow to Horsemarket, where the old market cross is situated – having been moved from the corner where Main Street turns into Market Street. Mill Brow descends steeply to the river, and here seven mill wheels once harnessed the water power of a small stream which is now covered over.

From the old market column, go through the narrow cobbled way to visit the fine Norman church. Dedicated to St Mary, the oldest parts are twelfth century and include three fine arches, and pillars of differing designs. The font, originally from the fourteenth century Killington chapel, has had a chequered history and was found being used as an animal trough on a local farm, before being restored to its present place and intended use earlier this century. The finely-carved oak pulpit is dated 1619.

Go to the far corner of the churchyard above the river and, a few paces along, to Ruskin's View. Turner visited the town in 1816 and from the corner of the churchyard made a sketch, the basis for a later water-colour. The octagonal building known as the

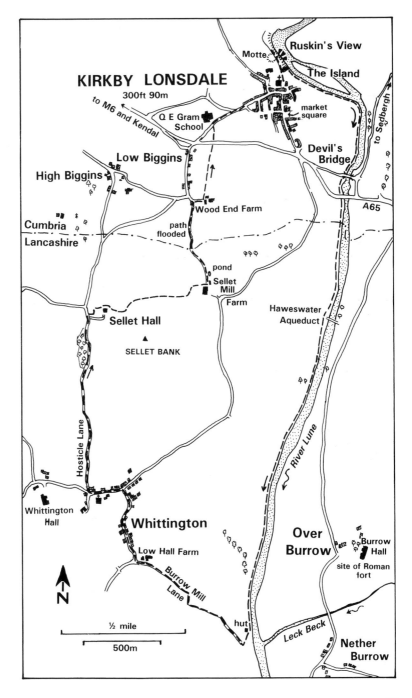

KIRKBY LONSDALE
300ft 90m

Ruskin's View

Motte

The Island

to M6 and Kendal

Q E Gram School

market square

to Sedbergh

Devil's Bridge

Low Biggins

High Biggins

Wood End Farm

A65

Cumbria

Lancashire

path flooded

pond

Sellet Mill Farm

Haweswater Aqueduct

Sellet Hall

SELLET BANK

River Lune

Hosticle Lane

Whittington Hall

Whittington

Over Burrow

Burrow Hall

Low Hall Farm

site of Roman fort

N

Burrow Mill Lane

½ mile

500m

hut

Leck Beck

Nether Burrow

The Church of St Mary, Kirkby Lonsdale.

gazebo features in the painting. The nine-teenth century art critic John Ruskin was captivated by the view:

'Whatever moorland, hill and sweet river and English forest foliage can be seen at their best is gathered there, and chiefly seen from the steep bank which falls to the stream side from the upper part of the town itself.'

Underley Hall is the large turreted building on the left. It was built in the 1820s and, from 1893 to 1939, came into the possession of Lord and Lady Cavendish-Bentinck, who became local benefactors.

A little further along the terrace, behind the wall, is Cockpit Hill, the now rather eroded motte and bailey of Norman times and in the eighteenth century the scene of cock-fighting. The vicarage is most famed for its occupant, the Rev Llewellyn-Davies and his five sons, who lived there from 1889 to 1908

and who inspired J M Barrie to write *Peter Pan*. Barrie took responsibility for the edu-cation of all five boys after both parents died young.

Return to the gazebo and descend the eighty-five Radical Steps to river level, turn-ing right along the riverside footpath to Devil's Bridge. There is a wealth of flowers by the river, including pink purslane, the delicate lesser stitchwort, sweet cicely, good king Henry and herb bennet. By the end of the summer there are swathes of the tall Himalayan balsam in two shades of pink, especially on the Island where the river divides, as well as the white-flowered, ram-pant Japanese knotweed. Two plants still in bloom into the autumn are red campion and herb robert, which have the longest flowering period of any British flower.

The Lune is noted for its salmon and trout, and attracts many anglers. Salmon come up

The thirteenth century Devil's Bridge spanning the River Lune has a strange legend attached to it.

the river in the autumn to breed, but they wait until there is a good depth of water. The river soon enters a wide rocky bed with tilted layers of limestone, where large oaks and elms line the bank and the famous Devil's Bridge comes into view. The bridge dates from the early thirteenth century – about 1230 – when there was much east-west traffic, as monastic herds of sheep went to mountain pastures in Cumberland. St Marys in York and Fountains abbeys each had an interest in replacing

a hazardous ford. In 1275 and 1365 there are records of tolls levied to raise money for bridge repairs. The bridge spans the river in three graceful, high, ribbed arches, supported on massive six-sided piers. In his now classic book *The Ancient Bridges of the North of England*, E Jervoise describes the Devil's Bridge as 'by far the finest bridge in the north of England'.

The odd name comes from a later legend in which a woman is separated from her cows by the flooded river. The devil offers to build a bridge in return for the soul of the first being to cross it, knowing that the woman's husband will be returning home. The woman agrees, but sends her dog over first, thereby defeating the devil. Today, the bridge is an ever-increasing attraction, particularly to motorcyclists and, occasionally, you may see a fearless youth leap from the parapet into the pool, forty-five feet (13.7m) below.

The new Stanley Bridge was built in 1932, to relieve the old one of heavy traffic, and was opened by Oliver Stanley, MP for Westmorland, after whom it was named. Continue along the right bank of a now mature River Lune, climbing up at the next bridge which carries the Haweswater aqueduct. The large volume of water which passes through these pipes on the way from the Lake District to Manchester does so in complete silence.

There is good birdwatching along this stretch of the river as it broadens out with large gravel banks and a sandy rivercliff. Four waders are attracted to the shingle banks: the oystercatcher, common sandpiper, redshank and curlew. Goosander, mute swan, mallard and shelduck take to the water and, in the breeding season, sandmartins, which nest in the dozens of holes excavated in the vertical riverbank, wheel and cry incessantly overhead.

Whittington church tower comes into view on the right and across on the other side of the river lies the hamlet of Over Burrow, a place of great historical interest. It is the site of the Roman fort of Calacum, a large military station founded by Agricola in AD 79 as he pressed through Brigantes country, northwards up the Lune Valley. It lies in a commanding, elevated position between the Leck and the Lune. A stone altar and a pendant of pure gold are among the findings. Borrow Hall, built in 1740, was erected on the site of part of the fort.

Turn up by the fisherman's hut and along the flowery, hedge-lined Borrow Mill Lane.

Whittington Races are held every Good Friday: the steeplechase crosses the lane, where jumps over the hedges have been permanently prepared. Enter the village at Low hall Farm, pass the Dragons Head, the village hall, former school, and many old cottages and houses. Turn left to the church of St Michael, which stands on a knoll in a fine position overlooking the river. The site is one of a motte and bailey castle, but the oldest part of the church is the tall fifteenth century tower. The church was largely restored in 1875.

Continue and turn right along the very narrow Hosticle Lane, past Lane House Farm and up the hill to Sellet Hall. Take the next right after the main entrance, which leads through the car park and past the visitor's entrance to the gardens, open to the public during the summer months. They include a herb garden, herbaceous borders and a woodland garden. The hall, a private house, has fine chimney stacks and parts of it date back to Tudor times.

Go on through a gate and left to follow the hedge. The rounded hill on the right is a glacial drumlin, where large limestone boulders are scattered. Pass through the gate, turning right after the second gate to the field corner at Sellet Mill Farm.

Turn left by the side of a chicken shed for the path to Low Biggins. On crossing the county boundary, from Lancashire into Cumbria, a stream runs right down the path where, in wet weather and in winter, wellies may be necessary. At the road, turn right through the farmyard, then left across the fields to come out at the grammar school. Queen Elizabeth's was founded in 1591 when a tiny school was situated on Mill Brow. Since 1848, the school has been on the present site and has expanded in recent years. It now takes boys and girls with a proportion of boarders.

Turn right to reach the centre of Kirkby Lonsdale.

WALK 2: BARBONDALE, EASE GILL AND LECK BECK

Start: Casterton.   Grid Ref: 625 797
Distance: 12 miles (19km)
OS Maps: Pathfinder 628 or OS Touring Map and Guide 6
Walking Time: 6½ hours

Leave a full day for this fairly long but most interesting walk. From Casterton it goes through the fields to Barbon, then up through the woods of Barbon Manor, climbing gently up the fellside to 1,000 feet (306m) at Bullpot of the Witches, where it enters one of the great caving districts of Britain. A little scrambling may be needed at Ease Gill Kirk but there follows a lovely walk down Leck Beck through woods to Cowan Bridge. Fields and lanes bring you back to Casterton. There is a large car park at the top of the hill, left of the main road, on the north side of Casterton village.

Casterton, as the name suggests, was a Roman camp on the military road which led north to Carlisle and Hadrian's Wall. Harry Speight, writing about 1890, poetically describes the village as lying 'almost hidden from view in a lovely dell formed by the murmuring rivulet which courses through its midst'. Astride the main road, it still occupies a favoured spot and retains the old-fashioned look of a peaceful English village. That is, until Casterton School starts its term. This fine boarding school for girls forms an important part of the community. It all began in 1823 as the little school for daughters of the clergy, in Cowan Bridge, which the Brontë sisters attended in 1824-25. It moved to Casterton a few years later. The Rev William Carus-Wilson of Casterton Hall not only founded Cowan Bridge School but, in 1838, was also responsible for building Casterton Church. He is said to be the model for Mr Brocklehurst in Charlotte Brontë's *Jane Eyre*.

The Pheasant Inn is a fine traditional pub with accommodation, and across the road is the scenic nine-hole golf course.

Start the walk by going north on the A683 in the Sedbergh direction and, at the top of the hill opposite the sports field, turn right along a narrow, hedge-lined lane. The variety of trees and shrubs in a hedge are a measure

of its age, so these hedges must be very old.

Cross the railway and go left as far as a farm track, then right, over a cattle grid and, after 35 yards (32m), left over a step stile to follow the wall to Fell Garth Farm. At the lane, turn right for a few paces then left through a gate to approach the left of Whelprigg Mansion.

The route crosses the drive, enshrouded in trees, where the nuthatch is one of the residents. This sleek-looking bird looks like a small woodpecker and, although it uses its bill to crack nuts and nests in holes in trees, it belongs to a family of which it is the only member to breed in Britain.

Go straight across a wide stretch of parkland, with scattered oak, ash and beech trees, to the far left corner and join a farm track which curves left. From here, there's a good view of Barbon Manor standing proudly on the hillside in the centre of a patch of woodland.

Just before the farm – Low Bank House – take the stile on the right, bearing half-left to a small gate which leads to the road. Over the road use the wooden gate, making for the far lowest corner and a kissing gate; cross the old railway again and enter the village of Barbon.

Barbon means farm by the spring, from its name in *Domesday Book* of 'Berebrune'. The village, of stone and white-washed cottages,

35

Barbon Church and beck.

has four or five narrow byroads leading to it, but it lies back from the main road and remains a quiet place. Pass the village hall, the friendly, cobble-fronted general store, and the reading room built in 1884, then turn right at the war memorial. Barbon Inn is noted for its good food, and nearby gardens are decorated with topiary, magnolias and statuary.

The attractive church, entered through a lych-gate, was built in 1892 under the care of the Rev James Harrison, who was vicar of Barbon for fifty-five years and who was held in awe by the villagers. It was he who founded

the reading room – as a community centre for men and boys. Today Barbon is the setting for an annual car and motor-cycle rally, courtesy of the owner of Barbon Manor.

Pass behind the church, along the road to Barbon Manor and over Barbon Beck – the fine red sandstone bridge is dated 1885. Follow the tarmac drive, leaving it at the fingerpost along a good woodland path. The impressive manor was built by the Kay-Shuttleworths as a Victorian retreat. Sir James, who introduced Charlotte Brontë to her biographer Mrs Gaskell, is considered the founder of English popular education.

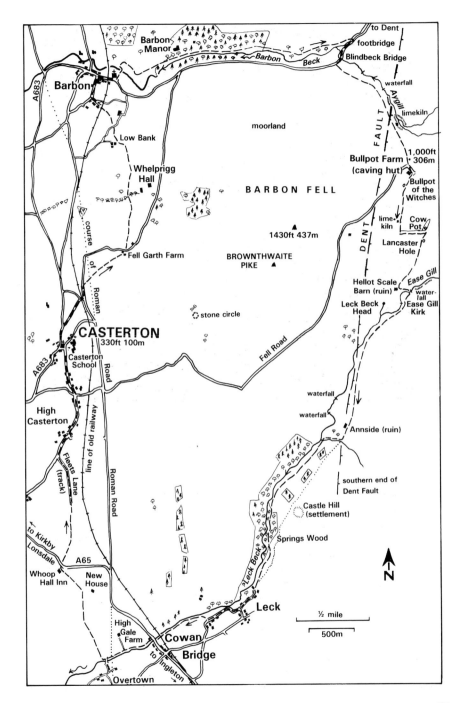

to Dent

footbridge

Blindbeck Bridge

waterfall

Barbon Manor

Barbon Beck

Barbon

A683

limekiln

moorland

Low Bank

F A U L T

Aygill

1,000ft
306m

Whelprigg Hall

B A R B O N   F E L L

Bullpot Farm
(caving hut)

Bullpot
of the
Witches

lime-
kiln

Cow
Pot

D E N T

Lancaster
Hole

1430ft 437m

Fell Garth Farm

course of

Roman

BROWNTHWAITE
PIKE

Hellot Scale
Barn (ruin)

Ease Gill

Leck Beck
Head

water-
fall

Ease Gill
Kirk

stone circle

CASTERTON
330ft 100m

Casterton
School

Fell Road

A683

Road

waterfall

High
Casterton

line of old railway

waterfall

Annside (ruin)

Fleets Lane
(track)

southern end of
Dent Fault

to Kirkby
Lonsdale

Roman Road

Castle Hill
(settlement)

A65

Springs Wood

Whoop
Hall Inn

New
House

Leck Beck

N

Leck

½ mile

500m

High
Gale
Farm

Cowan
Bridge

to Ingleton

Overtown

37

The track through the woods runs alongside the lively Barbon Beck which tumbles over bedrock of Silurian grits and slates, like those that outcrop on the path side. In the shelter of the trees a number of pheasants scuttle about, but in late summer this is a good place for fungi. The well-known fly agaric – red with white spots – and the unmistakeable stinkhorn grow here. Two bright orange ones are the false chanterelle and staghorn fungus, and none of these are for eating.

The path emerges onto a fellside with scattered trees. At this point keep an eye open for the buzzard which may be patrolling the steep sides of the dale. The kestrel and cuckoo also frequent this area.

The stream now becomes Barkin Beck, and along its banks grow alder, oak, ash, hawthorn and crab apple. The rocks in the beck dip upstream, the same Silurian slates and grits, but the Dent Fault, and limestone, is not far away. The fell on the right is Barbon Low Fell, ahead is Barbon High Fell and Crag Hill, while on the left are the slopes of Middleton Fell.

Cross the footbridge and turn right along the road, crossing the stone Blindbeck Bridge. The beckside is a popular place for motorists to stop and makes a good picnic spot. A few yards past the bridge, take the track to the left, aiming for a fold in the hills – between Barbon Low and High fells, where Aygill Beck descends over two scenic waterfalls. In the wet ground grow three -wort plants – butterwort, lousewort and lesser spearwort – and a close inspection will also reveal round-leaved sundew. *Wort* when attached to the name of a flower usually means it is good or worthy for something. For example, a cow that ate butterwort produced good butter. On the other hand lousewort was supposed to transmit lice to sheep. Spearwort has spear-shaped leaves that are poisonous, and the origin of its name may be lost.

A view left up Barbondale shows a smooth-sided, almost glacial U-shape. It is a fault-guided valley, excavated along the line of the Dent Fault, which here gives a small hiccup to one side as it leaves Barbondale and crosses the path higher up. By the time you arrive at the gate into the green lane you will have crossed the fault line and entered limestone country, an exciting part of the walk. The first indication is a rocky hollow over to the left occupied by a double limekiln.

The green lane leads to Bullpot Farm, a caver's hut and the highest point on the walk – 1,000 feet (306m). Pass through the yard and a gate, and not far along the track is Bullpot of the Witches, an impressive hole, fifty feet (15m) deep, which can be viewed with care. It may have water pouring down or it could be dry.

Pass another double limekiln and continue to the wall, turning left to visit Cow Pot in a small enclosure on the left. A stream disappears down enlarged and sculptured clefts in the limestone. A slab of rock makes a delicate natural bridge and the top of the pothole is decorated with ferns. Rare plants on the limestone of the area include rigid buckler fern, limestone polypody and mossy saxifrage.

Follow the valley down and, 100 yards (90m) along and just beyond an outcrop of limestone, is the manhole entrance to Lancaster Hole. Discovered in 1946, this chance find leads to very extensive passages, caves and grottos which contain some of the most beautiful formations in the country. The whole system of Easegill Caverns has twenty-eight miles (45km) of interconnected passages, the longest cave system in Britain and twelfth in the world. Surface water passes down fourteen major sinkholes and then travels through the network to a single outlet, the resurgence at Leck Beck Head.

Continue down the dry valley via a chain of grassy sinkholes and follow the wall over a knoll to the ruins of Hellot Scale Barn. In the distance on the left you can see the Three Men of Gragareth, stone towers silhouetted

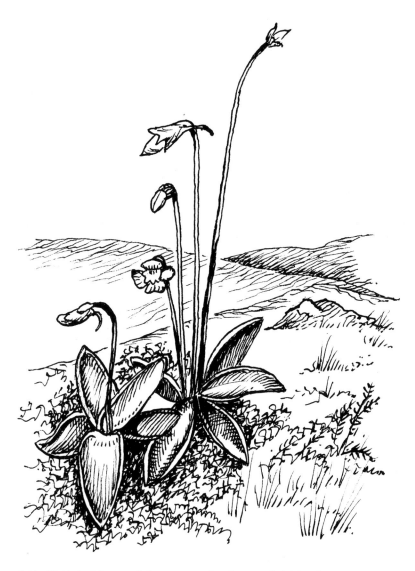

Butterwort is identified by its delicate purple flowers growing from the centre of a bright yellow-green rosette of sticky leaves.

on the skyline. Turn in the same direction, on a narrow path, to scramble across Ease Gill. Take great care on wet, slippery limestone. The stream bed is likely to be dry and you can explore the gorge of Upper Easegill Kirk, a boulder-strewn, thirty-foot (10m) deep hole with vertical limestone walls. The beck then makes a wide curve before entering the rock amphitheatre of Lower Ease Gill Kirk, where Witch's Cave can be explored from below, a great place for budding potholers.

Find a small path among the bracken, high on the left side of the gill, and join the right of way down the valley. The spring at Leck Beck Head is out of sight, but the gushing water can be seen near the junction with Ease Gill. Leck Beck now forms the county boundary and the next part of the route is in Lancashire.

Follow the top edge of the ravine for a splendid walk down Leck Beck. The beck follows the Dent Fault to its southern extremity near to Leck village. Amongst the heather, there are limestone scars on the hillside to the left, with outcrops of Silurian grits and slates in the bracken to the right. Gradually move away from the beck to pass the ruined farmhouse of Anneside, then at the next gully turn down, close to the stream, to regain the bank of Leck Beck, now a fine rushing river.

There follows an excellent section along the river, where you may see goosander and grey wagtail, which then leads into attractive deciduous woodland where, in the month of May, the bluebells form a riot of colour. Among the more common woodland plants are wood sanicle, wood forget-me-not, hairy rock-cress and eleven species of fern.

On reaching a group of cottages at Leck Mill, proceed along the road, fork right, and beyond a line of cottages in Leck village, turn right through a squeezer stile beneath a lone sycamore to regain the riverside once more. The path follows the beck, passes beneath the arches of the disused railway and comes out in Cowan Bridge.

Just over the old bridge, at Cowan Bridge is a cottage with a plaque which records that Maria, Elizabeth, Charlotte and Emily Brontë lived here as pupils of Rev Carus-Wilson's Clergy Daughters' School from 1824-25. It was portrayed as 'Lowood' in *Jane Eyre*. The school was moved to Casterton in 1833.

From the bridge in Cowan Bridge, continue the walk on the right bank. Look out for butterflies such as the peacock, small tortoiseshell and meadow brown among the riverside vegetation. At a cattle grid, turn away from the river through the fields, keeping right of a plantation along hedgerows to a small footbridge at the far end of a field, with New House on the right.

Cross the neat campsite and follow stiles diagonally through fields to the Whoop Hall Inn, its red ridge-tiles visible from a distance. Cross the busy A65 and proceed along the edge of three fields to Fleets Lane. The second field has woody nightshade and French cranesbill growing near the path. The blue-purple flowers of woody nightshade last through the summer and the berries are red. The large pink flowers of French cranesbill are garden escapes, though native in the Pyrenees.

Fleets Lane leads you back into Cumbria and High Casterton. Turn right on Chapelhouse Lane, past the golf course and some fine houses and gardens, to return to Casterton village.

WALK 3: BARBON AND MIDDLETON FELL

Start: Barbon. Grid Ref: 629 825
Distance: 13 miles (21km)
OS Maps: Pathfinder 628 or OS Touring Map and Guide 6
Walking Time: 6 hours

For those who like a good long walk, the round of Middleton Fell is an uninterrupted, bracing moorland circuit, and this is combined with a ramble through farmland along the Lune Valley. The walk begins in Barbon, visits the medieval, fortified Middleton Hall, includes an interesting botanical site, goes on to climb to 2,000 feet (609m) on Calf Top and a descends over Eskholme Pike and Devils Crag. There are excellent and changing views from the tops, and route-finding is not too difficult. There is parking space in front of Barbon village hall.

The spacious and attractive village of Barbon lies in a fine position on the side of the broad Lune Valley, at the foot of the fells and just off the main road from Kirkby Lonsdale to Sedbergh. A gap through the upland, along Barbon Beck, carries a narrow road from Barbon into the isolated valley of Barbondale and through into Dentdale.

Until 1963, the railway line from Ingleton to Tebay ran between the church and the post office in Barbon, but there is little sign of its former existence. Few tourists visit the village, which remains quiet and peaceful for most of the year until it is livened up, in June and July, by the annual car and motor-bike rallies.

From the memorial at the centre of the village, take the Sedbergh road, then go first right, opposite the Methodist chapel. The narrow road soon crosses Barbon Beck. Look over the bridge to see a fine outcrop of red conglomerate, looking like some giant pebbly concrete. This is a wedge of Carboniferous strata, here squeezed between Silurian slates which make up the fells on both sides of the valley.

About half a mile (800m) along the road, after passing the lane to Borwick Hall, take the stile (on the far side of a stream) to Borwens Farm, a Roman name meaning 'cairn' or 'pile of stones'. A lintel on the barn

is dated 1718. Go through the farmyard and on across a field, past a large oak. The hummocky ground on the right is the site of an ancient homestead. Approach close to the top end of a wood to cross a small stream and reach a lane leading to Sowermire Farm.

Pass under the old railway, here raised on an embankment, and after following it for 150 yards (140m) bear half-right to the top of a field, then cut up, past a barn, and along the edge of Sowermire Wood. Go through a green metal gate to keep above the barn and farm of Low Fellside.

As you make your way to Mill House Farm, across a large pasture, there are good views of the Lune Valley. You are likely to come across curlew, lapwing or oystercatcher, all of which like the rougher ground on the edge of the upland. In autumn there are large flocks of fieldfares which feed on haws and rowan berries. Among the Mill House group of buildings, you may see a charm of goldfinches. A close view of this colourful bird shows the bright yellow wing-patch and striking red, white and black head.

Cross the footbridge over the rushing Millhouse Beck to the lane and, 60 yards (55m) down it, turn through a squeezer stile to pass along a diagonal line of stone stiles across meadows and fields, passing finally under the old railway to Tossbeck Farm. On

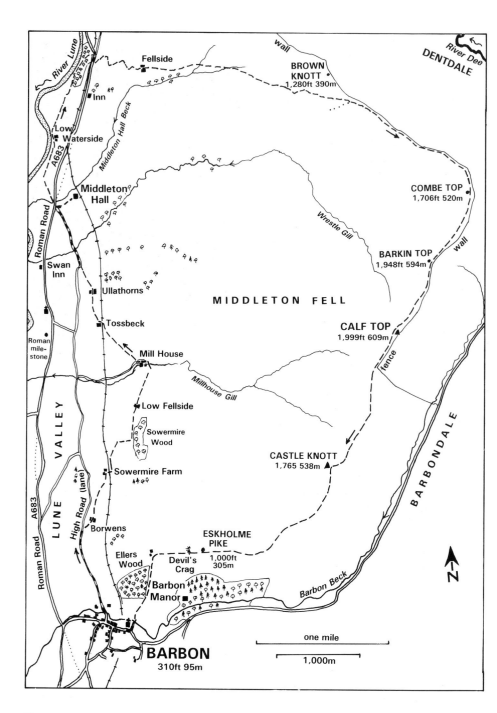

Fellside

BROWN
KNOTT •
1,280ft 390m

River Dee
DENTDALE

wall

River Lune

Inn

Middleton Hall Beck

Low
Waterside

A683

Roman Road

Middleton
Hall

COMBE TOP •
1,706ft 520m

Wrestle Gill

Swan
Inn

BARKIN TOP •
1,948ft 594m

wall

Ullathorns

MIDDLETON FELL

Roman
mile-
stone

Tossbeck

CALF TOP
1,999ft 609m

Mill House

fence

Millhouse Gill

VALLEY

Low Fellside

Sowermire
Wood

CASTLE KNOTT
1,765 538m ▲

BARBONDALE

A683

High Road (lane)

LUNE

Sowermire Farm

Borwens

ESKHOLME
PIKE

Roman Road

Ellers
Wood

Devil's
Crag

1,000ft
305m

Barbon
Manor

Barbon Beck

N

one mile

BARBON
310ft 95m

1,000m

42

the main road below Tossbeck is Middleton Church, built in 1634, and over to the left of it is a Roman milestone. The round sandstone pillar - as tall as a man – was erected on the hillside after its discovery in the 1830s. The lettering *MP LIII*, fifty-three Roman miles, is accepted as the distance to Carlisle.

Turn right through the farmyard (past a wall corner) and along to Ullathorns, a farm dated 1671. The projecting porch has an upper storey. Go through the farmyard and follow a ditch down to a gate, then go diagonally across a field to the old road from Barbon, a delightful narrow lane which leads over Stockdale Beck to the main road and Middleton Hall.

Take time to have a closer look at this fine medieval hall, the home of the powerful Middleton family who used to provide falcons for the lords of Kendal. Beyond walnut trees, an archway leads through the massive, fortified curtain wall, damaged by cannon fire in the Civil War, into a courtyard where the hall, almost in its original state, contains a fourteenth century low, arched passage, dividing the great hall from the kitchens and leading into an inner courtyard. The wall-cum-gatehouse is a scheduled ancient monument to which members of the public are allowed access.

The remains of the medieval curtain wall at Middleton Hall.

Returning to Middleton Hall Bridge, cross the bridge and turn left through a farm gate, diagonally across the upper part of the field to where the path follows the edge of a river terrace as it approaches the Lune. Along here you get the first view of the Howgills.

Pass to the immediate left of the farmhouse of Low Waterside, where there is a wonderful vista of a broad bend in the river, then follow along a hedge and ditch to a barn. Keeping the same direction, but a few paces to the right, pass a line of old hazels. The path goes alongside then enters a lovely patch of ancient deciduous woodland where ferns, bluebells, greater stitchwort, wood sorrel, water avens and red campion abound.

Ascend to the road, turn right and go up across the common, which is reserved as a gypsy encampment when the Appleby and Brough fairs are taking place. Zigzag or cut up more steeply across a hillside where betony, meadow vetchling, devilsbit scabious and dyers greenweed brighten the slopes. The last one of these is a small shrub, related to broom, from which a yellow dye is obtained. A green dye was first developed in Kendal in the fourteenth century, where cloth was first dyed yellow using dyers greenweed; it was then dipped in blue woad to produce a colour known as Kendal green.

Higher up, on the right of the tarred track, is an interesting botanical wet patch and a

In spring the lapwing is seen in an aerial display over its territory, rolling and twisting in a seemingly uncontrolled earthward plunge.

whole host of wet-loving plants, including common-spotted orchid, bog asphodel and marsh lousewort. But among them is the lovely northern plant, marsh cinquefoil – the name means five leaves – a member of the strawberry family, the deep reddish sepals and petals of which make it most distinctive.

Walk up through the windswept farm of Fellside to open, bracken-covered moorland. In the summer months you will have the meadow pipit for company as it twitters on

high before sideslipping through the air, wings outspread and tail up. A more musical song comes from the skylark which continues to sing as it drops earthward. This is the home, too, of the curlew, which prefers the lower fell slopes and, among rocky outcrops and old walls, the wheatear finds its favourite habitat.

Cross a ford, where the stream flows over well-cleaved Silurian slates and, following the well-worn, winding track for over a mile

(2km), climb gradually to a high point on the ridge, along which runs a major boundary wall. From here there are magnificent views back to the upper Lune Valley and gorge, down below to Sedbergh and the Rawthey Valley, with Dentdale immediately below and Garsdale behind. Between these dales are the heights of the Howgills, Baugh Fell and Rise Hill.

Continue along the wall, for about two miles (3km), to Calf Top – 1,999 feet (609m) above sea level. The wall here follows the boundary of the National Park, though the path stays outside it. The first steep climb is up to Combe Top immediately above Combe Scar (*walk 5*), visible from Gawthrop and Dent. Whernside and Crag Hill come into view, before one disappears behind the other. From the high point of Barkin Top there is not much more climbing to the trig point on Calf Top, from where Ingleborough is visible.

Leave Calf Top, then the reassuring wall and fence, to dip down and up to the cairn on Castle Knott. Try to keep to the worn path. (In mist take a bearing of 210° from north.) Over to the left there is a dramatic view into Barbondale, a valley which runs along the Dent Fault. It was along here that Adam Sedgwick came one winter's night on his way home from Cambridge. He took a post-chaise from Kirkby Lonsdale, but it was so dark and misty the driver lost the 'road' (only wheel tracks) several times. In the end Sedgwick, taking one of the lamps, led the driver and horses the seven miles (11km) into Dent: 'All bespattered with sleet and snow I looked like an old grizzly watchman'.

From Castle Knott go straight on down the mat grass-covered slope. Ahead you can see the white building of Bullpot Farm (*walk 2*), the cavers' hut, with Pendle Hill above it and Barbon Fell straight across. As you curve round to the right – between two cairns – there are views of the meandering Lune below Kirkby Lonsdale, Morecambe Bay is spread out like a map, and further right is the long profile of the Lakeland mountains.

Follow the middle of the ridge, gradually descending to Eskholme Pike, where a square stone tower stands on a rocky crag with more extensive views up and down the Lune Valley. Immediately below is Devils Crag, a jutting cliff of more Silurian rock, and a steep drop down to a gate under sycamores. The slopes are dotted with little tufts of the pale green lichen, *Cladonia*, a kind of reindeer moss. Cross the field to a gate above the corner of Ellers Wood and enter a parkland of scattered oaks, part of Barbon Manor estate, entering Barbon village by the attractive Victorian church.

WALK 4: SEDBERGH TO DENT OVER FROSTROW FELL

Start:	Sedbergh. Grid Ref: 657 921
Distance:	11 miles (17½ km)
OS Maps:	Outdoor Leisure 2 or Yorkshire Dales Touring Map 6
Walking Time:	6 hours

Set aside a full day for this walk from Sedbergh to Dent and back. It passes over the rough fells of Frostrow, and returns by a stretch of the River Dee and a short climb back over to Millthrop. There are fine views and a variety of flora and fauna to look out for. The attractive village of Dent with its old-fashioned charm is the main aim of the walk. Map and compass will be useful in poor weather. There is good parking in Sedbergh.

Part of Cumbria since 1974, Sedbergh is the largest town within the Yorkshire Dales National Park. Its market charter dates from 1251, and hand-knitted woollens became an established trade. In the 1790s it entered an industrial phase with the building of cotton mills at Howgill, Birks and Millthrop. The woollen mill at Hebblethwaite Hall was later succeeded by Farfield Mill on the River Clough. Sedbergh grew in size and importance, and many of the houses and cottages date from this period, including the cobbled yards off Main Street such as Weavers Yard, Kings Yard and Davis Yard. Railton Yard, approached from Back Lane, still has its spinning gallery. The town now finds it has considerable advantages for developing the tourist trade.

Sedbergh's public school has brought prosperity and fame to the town. Its most distinguished ex-pupil was Adam Sedgwick, professor of geology at Cambridge, and the poet Wordsworth sent his son to Sedbergh. 'It is Cautley, Calf and Winder, that makes the Sedbergh man' says the school song and, no doubt, training on the Howgills contributed to the school's present fame as the provider of great Rugby Union players throughout the land.

If, while wandering through Sedbergh on a sunny day, you cast your eyes upwards, you may see a party of swifts circling round in a screaming frenzy, a sure sign of the fullness of summer. They are only with us for sixteen weeks and leave for southern Africa early in August, a 5,000 mile (8,000km) journey which takes a month. When they return in the spring they will use the same nests and pair with the same mate as the previous year. During their long life – twelve or thirteen years is not unusual – they seldom land, except to visit their nests. You can see them from the Loftus Hill car park as they enter or leave the eaves of the old grammar school.

Walk along Main Street past the National Park visitor centre, and turn right at the end past the playing fields and over the hill, branching right at the stile to reach Mill Bridge over the River Rawthey. The mill, which was built on the north side of the river, was destroyed by fire in the late 1940s and is now a group of private dwellings.

Cross the bridge, and turn left for a few yards along a delightful stretch of river, then right, up a passage between the cottages of Millthrop. Turn left along the road for 165 yards (150m), then go right, at a footpath sign, up a narrow walled track. At the metal gate take the stile to the left of it, through the fields (the next stile is in the third field at its bottom corner) to a farm track, following it to Hollins Lane.

Turn right to the end of the lane, past Low and High Hollins – the word means 'holly'. The last group of buildings is Side Farm, where you emerge onto the open moor of Frostrow Fell – 'Frosti's nook of land'. In wet places by the path, tiny plants of sundew grow and, on the fell, you are likely to be accompanied by the call of the curlew and the skylark's outpouring of song. Take care in misty weather, and make use of map and compass. The general bearing is 120° from north.

Follow the well-trodden bridleway along a ridge from which there are good views of the Howgill summits and of Baugh Fell ahead. After half a mile (800m), Holebeck Gill appears to the left. Follow alongside it, then leaving its gathering grounds on the left, climb steadily to follow a wall to the highest point of 950 feet (290m) and, on a clear day, a panoramic view. To the rear is the skyline of the Lakeland mountains and the Howgills, and ahead are Whernside, Dentdale, the flat-topped profile of Crag Hill with Combe Scar, and the hummocky outline of Middleton Fell on its right.

Follow the wall and the sign 'BW Lunds' to a green lane. After 130 yards (120m) along the lane, go through a metal gate on the left and follow the wall, then Blea Beck Gill, down to two hen-huts. At this point go left, through the fields, to High Hall.

The route is not easy to follow, and this is where you play 'hunt the stile'. In the third field aim for the tall fencing post and then, ignoring the slab bridge over the stream, continue, right, up the slope to a stile beyond some oak trees. Go along the broad ridge and another stile is hidden in a group of trees on the right. The barn ahead is the abandoned farm of Thackthwaite. Go round the left of the building, then between two walls to an almost-hidden stile opposite a small barn, leading through three fields to High Hall.

This ancient farmhouse is dated 1625 and probably replaced a much older building. It

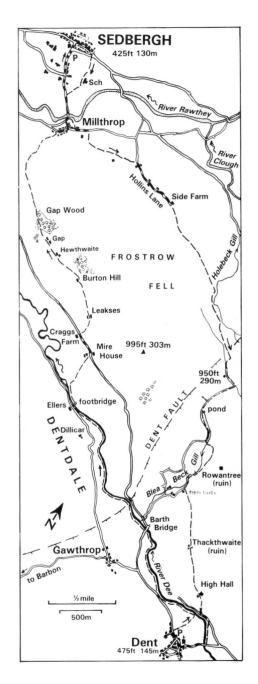

was a home of the Sill family for a time and is said to be Emily Brontë's model for *Wuthering Heights*. Visitors are welcome at High Hall to see not only the interesting building, but also some of the rare breeds of animals being kept there.

High Hall has two fine chimneys.

Continue down the farm track, left along the tarred lane and over the stile to the River Dee and Church Bridge. From here it is just a short stroll into Dent, a small, compact village with narrow, winding cobbled streets, pubs, whitewashed cottages and a fine old church. Two large hunks of Shap granite in the main street, one set in the other, commemorate the great geologist Adam Sedgwick, born at the old parsonage by the green.

The village is also famous for its marble and its 'terrible knitters'. On the chancel floor of the church, you can examine some of the marble, actually a polished limestone containing fossil corals and crinoids. The crinoids are seen in the lighter grey stone but only the stems are present – in dozens of cross-section views. Marble was cut and polished in Dentdale factories and made into tables, fireplaces and ornaments, much in vogue in Victorian times. Dent is also famous for its knitting. The 'terrible knitters' – 'terrible' here being dialect for remarkable – were immortalised by Robert Southey in a book of tales. In order to protect the beauty of the village, Dent has been made a conservation area.

Just past the National Park car park, turn right to reach the riverbank. For the next two miles (3.2km), the walk follows a lovely scenic riverside footpath down the left bank of the River Dee past Barth Bridge to the footbridge at Ellers. The bank has been raised and reinforced to cope with the flooding which has long been a problem in this part of the dale.

Dentdale is notable for its hedgerows, but it also has some fine trees which, when standing alone, can grow into handsome shapes – including mature sycamores and elms. A field of bistort, that leafy plant with tall, pink flower spikes, is a reminder that its young leaves were once used to make the traditional Easter-ledge pudding. Culpeper, an early herbalist, recommended bistort as a cure for toothache.

Cross the footbridge at Ellers – meaning 'alders' – and go left for a short way on the other bank, before turning up to the road. Among the black-headed gulls, pied wagtails, dippers, herons and curlews that like to visit the river, the oystercatcher nests here by making a scrape in the shingle to lay its eggs. Its black and white plumage, pink legs and red bill make it most distinctive. It is only during this century that the oystercatcher has taken to breeding away from the coast. Probing for worms in a meadow is not much different from probing for worms on mudflats by the sea. Most recently, this opportunist has taken to nesting in meadow grass.

Turn left along the road, where Mire House is dated 1635, to another old farm – Crag Farm – 300 yards (175m) along on the left. Turn right here to Leakeses – where the Leake family once lived – a whitewashed farm

The old farming methods: haytime in Dentdale in the 1990s.

on the hillside. Go in front of the farmhouse and through the metal gate opposite a barn. Pass through the cobbled farmyard of Burton Hill, said to have once been an inn on an old packhorse route which ran high on this side of the valley. There was a building here in 1550, and the present one contains two ancient cupboards, one dated 1651.

On the right is the bluebell wood of Hewthwaite. Go round the front of Hew-thwaite Farm and through a gate to Gap Farm. Pass along the lower edge of Gap Wood, with more bluebells and a rookery high above. Listen for the woodpecker as it hammers away at dead bark to get at insects.

Exit from the wood along a good track, walled to start with. Down below, by the river, is Rash Mill, a 200 year old corn mill, still with its waterwheel intact which was last in use in the 1950s.

Curve right, over the shoulder of the hill, down to Millthrop. The view from this hillside contrasts the rounded Howgills (of Silurian grits and slates) and the horizontal scars and flat-topped hills (of Carboniferous limestone), with the Rawthey Valley between them (the line of the Dent Fault).

Pass through the village of Millthrop, turning left and right, to Mill Bridge, and end with a stroll up the road into Sedbergh.

WALK 5: GAWTHROP, COMBE SCAR AND FLINTERGILL

Start: Dent.   Grid Ref: 705 870
Distance: 5 miles (8km)
OS Maps: Outdoor Leisure 2 or Landranger 98
Walking Time: 3 hours.

Here is a lovely and varied walk that climbs gently up from Dent, through the pretty hamlet of Gawthrop, then passes two long-abandoned farmhouses and the glacial corrie below Combe Scar. A glimpse of Barbondale and a stroll along Occupation Road brings you to the steep descent of richly-wooded Flintergill. There are magnificent views, a variety of habitats for birds and flowers, and a flavour of the fells without needing to climb too high. Dent has an excellent car park.

The small, compact village of Dent has a charm and intimacy that lingers in the memory: the winding cobbled streets, white-washed houses, the chunk of pink granite and the interesting old church; the pubs, art galleries, shops and restaurants. The Sun Inn is 250 years old where the sign reads 'Best ale under the sun' and the George and Dragon competes for good food. The large twelfth century church is in a superb setting on a high point, so that seen from the river it dominates the view of the stone-flag roofed village. Dedicated to St Andrew, it contains much seventeenth century woodwork and the floor of the chancel is made of varieties of Dent marble. It was restored in the seventeenth century and considerably renovated in 1889.

Dent is known to its older inhabitants as Dent Town, distinguishing it from Dent, the dale. After the poet Hartley Coleridge (the

Dent Town from Church Bridge. The large church dominates the view of the stone-flag roofed village.

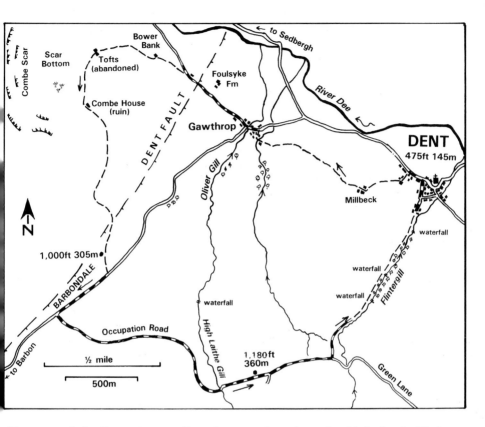

eldest son of the Romantic poet Samuel Taylor Coleridge) visited Dent, he wrote the poignant lines:

> 'There is a town of little note or praise;
> Narrow and winding are its rattling
>   streets,
> Where cart with cart in cumbrous
>   conflict meets;'

Adam Sedgwick also wrote of Dent and his childhood memories of the 1790s. He tells of the trade in wool, the life of the handknitters and the wooden galleries that jutted out, so that 'some of them almost shut out the sight of the sky from those who travelled along the pavement'.

From the National Park information board,

go down the road and left after the Wesleyan chapel, dated 1834, and through the farmyard. The sign to Gawthrop takes you through Millbeck Farm and over Mill Beck Hill. Gawthrop, meaning 'outlying farm of the cuckoos', soon became a hamlet, and from the fifteenth century had a corn mill which was in operation until 1876 when it was dismantled.

Go down through the village and left, past the end of the Barbon road. Where the road starts to descend, go through the gate on the left signed 'Stone Rigg 1½', past Bower Bank with good views down Dentdale, and the Howgill Fells partly hidden by Frostrow Fell. In spring, fields here are white with pignut and the redstart may give itself away by its *weet* call.

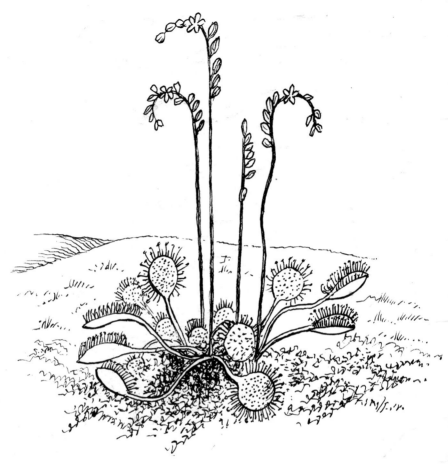

The insect-eating sundew favours damp hollows or wet patches. Many plants are only half this size.

Continue to Tofts farmhouse, which is still in one piece but abandoned. Go straight through the often muddy farmyard and over the stream by a small stone bridge. The route then follows the wheel tracks up the hillside to the left below some ash trees, to the ruins of Combe House, with the dark heights of Combe Scar rising up behind. Look out for birds such as the peregrine or buzzard which make use of the thermals in this wild place.

The word Combe is thought to come from an old Middle English word meaning 'peat dust'.

Combe House, now ruined and inhabited by jackdaws and swallows, dates from the mid-seventeenth century, and had fine stone-mullioned windows and an interesting double chimney-stack.

From here, a few steps towards the Scar brings a view of the broad, rounded hollow of a glacial corrie. The huge, steep-backed, amphitheatre-shaped bowl faces north, and ice must have hung around here long after it melted in the valleys (*see diagram on page 89*). In the wet ground near the large boulder (which bears an inscription) grow two insect-eating plants. The sticky, bright yellow-green leaves of butterwort curl at the edges, ready to clutch at an insect, and the flowers are an attractive deep purple on leafless stems. The tiny reddish plants of round-leaved sundew have their leaves covered in red hairs, each tipped with a shining droplet. Midges mistake the sticky glue for water in which to lay their eggs and are easily caught; white flowers appear in summer. Other flowers include lousewort, marsh valerian, birdseye primrose and occasional orchids.

Continuing along the same track on a gentle upward gradient: there are superb views of Dent Town and upper Dentdale with Rise Hill behind. Silurian slates outcrop along the way, ancient hawthorns dot the hillside and the cuckoo proclaims its territory.

On approaching a wall, curve left to a ladder stile. The green ridge ahead is on the limestone of Stone Rigg so, somewhere near the wall, you crossed the Dent Fault. The ridge on the right is Middleton Fell with Barbon Fell ahead. Pass to the left of a limekiln, the inner walls of which still have a lining of clinker, ash that has melted in the heat and produced a glassy coating. This indicates the sort of heat attained in the lime-making process. The resulting quicklime was slaked (by adding water) and mainly used to sweeten acid soils but was also needed to make mortar for building.

On reaching Barbondale Road, turn right for 500 yards (450m), getting an impression of the depth and narrowness of this valley, and go left on the 'green' Occupation Road. This road was largely used for transporting Dent marble, stone and coal along the margin of the valley. The highest point of the walk is reached near the crossing of High Laithe Gill, a dip in the road, at about 1,180 feet (360m). On the left is a large slab of Dent marble, not really a marble but a crinoidal limestone, which has some fine glacial scratches on its upper surface. It was probably quarried nearby and never removed. The stone quarry further on, opposite a branching green road to the right, was for sandstone, used in the extensive wall-building of the 1850s. Look across to Rise Hill where there are at least twenty stone walls on its flanks, rising to the summit ridge as if they were drawn with a ruler. They are a result of the 1856 enclosure by agreement, the last in the Dales.

Turn left down to Flintergill , an attractive deep gorge in ancient woodland. The trees include oak, elm, ash hazel and rowan, while at ground level the oniony smell and white flowers of wild garlic seems to dominate. After heavy rain, the gill has some impressive waterfalls. The steep path down leads through a pretty corner of Dent.

WALK 6: DEEPDALE FROM DENT

Start: Dent. Grid Ref: 705 870
Distance: 7½ miles (12km)
OS Maps: Outdoor Leisure 2 or Landranger 98
Walking Time: 4 hours

Dent makes a good starting point for exploring the beautiful little enclave of Deepdale, where there is a farm that owned slaves, a succession of miniature waterfalls, outstanding Dales scenery and a wonderful riverside walk. There is an excellent car park in Dent.

The fine church of Dent dates back to Norman times, around 1080, when the parish was under the care of Coverham Abbey in Wensleydale. It was rebuilt in 1417 and the chancel was added in the 1770s. The Norman tower fell down and was rebuilt in 1787, and the clock dates from 1828. In the church grounds is the old grammar school building, founded in 1604, and closed in 1898. The new school now serves as the village hall.

There once stood a market cross near to the present day fountain at the centre of the village. Dent Fair was held each June when the whole place became packed with people and stalls.

In 1854 a pauper of Dent, known as Old Willan, inherited a large sum of money from one Thomas Spooner, who had made his fortune in London. As soon as the news came, the church bells rang, but Old Willan kept to his odd ways, always wearing his night cap.

Start by going down to Church Bridge over the River Dee and continue along the road past the 'Dulux house' (Shoolbred – old English meaning 'narrow strip of land'). You may recognise this attractive farmhouse which was given a free coat of paint in return for using its pictures in TV adverts. At the milestone – six miles to Sedbergh – turn left up the lane to Hall Bank. In spring and summer look out for the rare, deep-red blooms of dusky cranesbill which grows in the

lane. The colour is very unusual and the petals are often drawn back like a dart. The next mile (1.5km) of the walk passes through a line of old farmhouses along the side of Dentdale, from where there are excellent views of the dale and of the entrance to Deepdale. The farms have lovely names, but do not advertise the fact.

For over 100 years until 1852, Hall Bank was the workhouse for Dent. Founded by the Quaker, Thomas Thistlethwaite, it housed up to fifty paupers – men, women and children. Turn right between the buildings, along by a wall and up a farm track, to Well Head where a lintel built into the barn reads RET 1681. The next group of cottages is on Backstone Gill where 'bake stones' were once collected, being ideal for the floor of the oven in which bread was baked.

Go over the footbridge, and wend your way in front of the Backstone Gill farmhouse and to the rear of the modern house. By a new plantation of saplings, pass below Scotchergill and Low Chapel, then above High Chapel. Local historian David Boulton suggests this is the site of a battle where, in 1534, local tenants of Coverham Abbey fought as they were dispossessed of their lands, against twenty men armed with bows, arrows, swords and shields.

On the hillside past High Chapel are the ruins of Green Rigg, an old farmhouse which now has trees growing out of it. Carry on in front of the next farm, Peggleswright, to

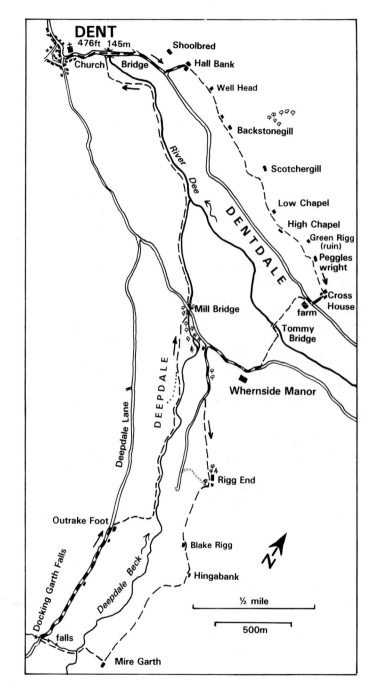

DENT
476ft 145m
Shoolbred
Church Bridge
Hall Bank
Well Head
Backstonegill
Scotchergill
River Dee
Low Chapel
High Chapel
Green Rigg (ruin)
Peggles wright
DENTDALE
Cross House
Mill Bridge
farm
Tommy Bridge
Deepdale Lane
DEEPDALE
Whernside Manor
Rigg End
Outrake Foot
Blake Rigg
Docking Garth Falls
Deepdale Beck
Hingabank
½ mile
N
falls
500m
Mire Garth

Cross House, a group of cottages. Go down the lane to the road, turn right, then left through the farmyard and down the side of a field, past a line of bird-cherry trees to reach Tommy Bridge. The wooden footbridge takes you back over the River Dee, from which point turn left then right along an ancient lane to the road on the south side of the dale.

Turn right, passing Whernside Manor, which was built by the Sill family in the eighteenth century using slave labour and money made from Jamaican slave plantations, then left up Dyke Hall Lane past the Methodist chapel, built in 1889. The lane leads into Deepdale and serves Rigg End Farm. Along the lane, among the cow parsley and pignut, look for wood sanicle, another member of the parsley family, which has such tight, button-like flowerheads that it always looks as if it is just about to open.

Go through (or over) a metal gate under a holly tree on the left, and head diagonally up the steep hillside for the clump of tall trees. A stile in the wall is overshadowed by a fine lime tree with its thin, pale-green leaves; the flowers come out in July and make good honey. Rigg End Farm, sheltered by a group of trees, stands high on the side of Deepdale, with extensive views.

The Benthams farmed Rigg End for generations, and descendants still talk of the Negro slaves kept on the farm here, and who were used for building Whernside Manor

Shoolbred – the 'Dulux house' – sits below Rise Hill near Dent.

Looking down Deepdale from Blake Rigg.

(when it was known as West House), a barn and a cottage. Family tradition suggests they lived in a cellar under an outhouse, connected to the farmhouse by a secret passage, which became haunted by dead slaves. It is also said that slaves were retained illegally for a few years after slavery was abolished. Black Dub – meaning 'black pool' – in Deepdale Beck is thought to be where they washed, or perhaps where one of them fell in love with one of Sill's daughters.

From Rigg End, now the only working farm on this side of Deepdale, descend a few paces down the farm track, and go left through a gate and some fields. Then, near a limekiln, join a double track to the rear of Blake Rigg, past a ruin and on to Hingabank

('steep bank'). Drop down past a barn and over a stream, rounding a second barn on the lower side and on in the up-dale direction to Mire Garth, now a holiday cottage.

The route now turns across the dale to the waterfalls and gorges of Gastack Beck. Ignoring the concrete drive, walk down the field wall to the beck. Turn upstream a few yards to a stile, cross Deepdale Beck and go up the sidestream – Gastack Beck. Explore a small limestone gorge to see a lovely waterfall. A little higher upstream is a vertical cave entrance and another miniature gorge with a deep pool.

Arrive on Deepdale Lane to see the most impressive of the little waterfalls, known as Docking Garth Falls. It is surrounded by tall

57

cliffs, has a deep plunge pool below it and is easily seen by passers-by on the road. To the left is a bank which makes a good picnic spot. Early purple orchids grow here among the outcrops of limestone, and a little further upstream is another waterfall; if you look downstream over the bridge parapet, there is a fourth. Gastack Beck flows in a hanging valley, and the series of waterfalls are where the valley 'hangs' above Deepdale.

Walk down Deepdale Lane for just over half a mile (1km), past Pocklesyke to Outrake Foot. Turn right down through the farm, on a concrete track, to the beck. The next mile (1.6km) is along the left bank of the delightful tree-lined beck, through flower-rich hay meadows. In May the lovely purplish-blue flowers of wood cranesbill add a distinctive colour as well as a name to these cranesbill meadows, noted for their rich variety of species. The beck runs on a bed of rock, and at a crossing point the stepping stones are the natural blocks of a limestone pavement with spaces between them where the water flows. Look out for dippers and grey wagtails along the beck, and overhead you may see swallows mobbing a sparrowhawk.

Keep straight on to where the dale gradually opens out and the Howgill Fells come into view ahead. After merging with a path from the left near a limekiln, notice a stone shed and ruined barn in a large field. Halfway across this field, turn down to some tall trees to find a path to the beck and Mill Bridge. Orange-tip butterflies frequent the riverside in May and June. Only the male has the orange tips to the forewings, and the female could be confused with the green-veined white which also occur here.

Cross the road and continue on the same bank, signed 'Church Bridge'. Soon Deepdale Beck joins the River Dee and, after a dry period, either of these watercourses can perform a disappearing act and run underground, leaving the riverbed completely dry. Up to the left is a good view of the Megger Stones which stand out on the shoulder of Crag Hill, similar to those which overlook Grisedale. Mike Harding suggests they could be of Celtic origin with a religious significance. Turn right at the gate, and continue downstream past the new cricket field to the bridge and up the road back into Dent.

WALK 7: MID-DENTDALE FROM IBBETH PERIL

Start: Ibbeth Peril car park. Grid Ref: 742 865
Distance: 3 miles (5km)
OS Maps: Outdoor Leisure 2 or Landranger 98
Walking Time: a leisurely 2 hours

A perfect introduction to Dentdale, this short walk visits historic farmhouses on both sides of the dale, provides extensive views for a minimum of effort and considers the limestone gorge of the capricious River Dee. The car park is on the north side of the valley 2½ miles (4km) up the dale from Dent, towards the Hawes-Ingleton road. It is recognisable by a footpath signpost on the roadside, and stone chippings.

Dentdale is noted for its farmhouses which are dotted evenly, every 200 to 300 yards (180-275m), along the lower slopes of both sides of the valley. This scattered distribution is in sharp contrast to other dales, such as Wharfedale, where all the farms are in villages first settled by the Anglians. It was the Norse settlers who came to Dentdale – in the tenth century. They preferred upland pastures for their sheep. Each farmstead, tucked into the shelter of a side gill, is separated from the next by a stretch of moorland.

The dale became prosperous through its farming and knitting. But it also had other industries. It was known for its butter-making, salted in casks made by coopers in the Dale. It had quarries for stone and marble, coal pits and its own corn mills.

Dentdale is steep-sided and narrow, and the River Dee has cut deep into its valley floor, creating a gorge in the solid rock. At the rear of the parking area is a footbridge, known as Nelly Bridge, where you can inspect the miniature canyon in the Great Scar limestone. In summer the river more or less dries up, leaving just a few pools, and it is possible to explore the riverbed.

To begin the walk, start off through the trees – in the direction of Dent – down the right bank of the river, to see the waterfall of Ibbeth Peril, 100 yards (90m) along, with its lovely plunge pool and gorge below. In spring,

a variety of wild flowers brighten the little path through the trees: bluebells, sweet woodruff, wood anemone, pignut and goldilocks among them. The last one is a delightful member of the buttercup family, with narrowly-divided leaves on the stem and usually only two or three golden-yellow petals. The Victorian writer Harry Speight calls it 'Ibby Peril' and notes the place is haunted by an uncanny little witch, frequently seen in the vicinity, her wizened features half hidden by a black bonnet.

Below Ibbeth Peril there are other hidden delights in the limestone riverbed. Off the route of this walk and a quarter of a mile (400m) downstream is an impressive cave in the side of the gorge and another fall; then roughly opposite Gibbs Hall is the waterfall and pool of Hell's Cauldron, above which is the exit of Hacker Gill which issues from a hole in the rockface into the gorge. In *The Rural Life of England*, published in 1844, William Howitt describes Hell's Cauldron in some detail:

'for the river here, overhung and dark, passes over some huge steps of the stony bed into a deep and black abyss, where the rending of the rocks and washing up of heaps of debris, shew with what fury the cauldron boils. . . . Yet fearful as this Hell's Cauldron must be when the stream is swollen, we are

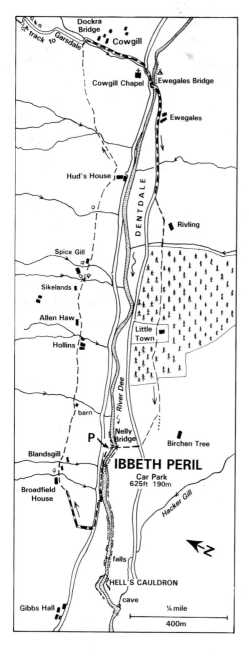

told that a boy once slipped in, and was carried through it, and washed up on the bank below, unhurt.'

From Ibbeth Peril waterfall, step up onto the road by the end of a wall and, after 250 yards (230m) in the same direction, turn right up a walled lane (signed Cowgill ¼) to Broadfield House. Pass in front of the farmhouse and behind the next two cottages – a converted barn, then Blandsgill. The incongruous frontage of Broadfield House comprises a Georgian extension to the seventeenth century farmhouse. For a time, one of the early owners of Stonehouse marble works (at Arten Gill) lived here. David Boulton in *Discovering Upper Dentdale* tells us that Blands was the home of Thomas and Ann Salkeld. A joiner and Quaker, Thomas was sent to prison for refusing to pay the vicar's 'Easter Reckonings'. After running the farm single-handed for two years, Ann Salkeld died, as did her two children, before Thomas was released.

Drop down through a gate gap to a barn and cattle grid, crossing the beck to pass behind the white-painted Hollins. Making use of the pure spring water from high on the fellside, a small brewery has been established here and Dent bitter is on sale in local bars.

Continue along the same level past the cottage of Alan Hawe, down a stretch of farm track and well below the white farmhouse of Sikelands (dated 1706) to a stone slab footbridge, hidden among sycamore trees. The next cottage is Spice Gill and an old lintel over the door reads 'M:1678'. The farm was called Spitegill in 1613 and is thought to have been named by a Norseman called Spytr. In the 1720s it belonged to Elizabeth Mason, a beautiful twenty year old heiress who in 1727 married Richard Thistlethwaite, son of William of Harbourgill (*see walk 13*).

Continue through fields to the farm Hud's House with its fine early seventeenth century chimney. In the 1680s, when it was known as

Artengill viaduct and Cowgill church, Dentdale.

Hudsfoss, James Mason lived here and provided a kind of bunkhouse in a hay loft for poor travellers to spend the night. Turn diagonally away from the farm and gently up through stiles to a walled green lane and Dockra Bridge. The lane is an old road over to Garsdale. There are some fine old cherry trees in Gill Wood just up the road.

From Dockra Bridge go down the lane to the road, to Cowgill Bridge and Chapel. The bridge contains a stone which declares 'this bridge repaired at the charge of the West Riding AD 1702'. The simple chapel in its idyllic setting has had quite a history. The foundation stone was laid by geologist Adam Sedgwick and the new church called Cowgill Chapel. Later, a curate renamed it Kirkthwaite as he thought Cowgill too vulgar.

Sedgwick was furious at the taking and misspelling of the local name Kirthwaite, and put all his efforts into getting the proper name of Cowgill restored. Queen Victoria and Gladstone were both involved, and in 1869 Parliament changed it back to Cowgill Chapel. *Adam Sedgwick's Dent* is a reprint of his classic Dales history which includes an account of the controversy.

Walk down the road and cross Ewegales Bridge. The bridge, along with Lea Yeat Bridge, was replaced after being destroyed in the floods of 1870. Below Ewegales Farm is the site of Dee Mill, a textile mill destroyed by fire early this century. The byroad on this side of the dale is a delightful country lane where meadow cranesbill and giant bellflower decorate the hedgerows. After a quarter of a

Cottages in mid-Dentdale.

mile (400m) along it, turn up to the left through a metal gate (signed 'Laithbank 1') to Rivling. This old farmhouse is said to have been a place where butter tubs were made. 'Rivling' means rivulet.

Enter the conifer plantation for a short way, pass in front of Little Town, where a George Burton lived as long ago as the 1650s, and pass through another stand of spruce trees. The trees give such dense shade that the ground beneath them is dead and the path stays wet for much of the year. A couple of fields further, turn down the concrete track to the road where there is a Victorian letterbox by the gate. Cross the road to return to Nelly Bridge and the car park.

WALK 8: UPPER DENTDALE AND THE CRAVEN WAY

Start: Lea Yeat.   Grid Ref: 761 869
Distance: 10 miles (16km)
OS Maps: Outdoor Leisure 2 or Landranger 98
Walking Time: 5 hours

A superb full day's walk takes in the upper reaches of the River Dee, a moorland stretch along the line of the Blea Moor tunnel (Settle-Carlisle line), a length of the old packhorse route of the Craven Way and returns along a string of farms in Dentdale. It ascends to nearly 1,800 feet (450m) on the slopes of Whernside and has one or two steep climbs. Lea Yeat is four miles (6.5km) up the dale from Dent. Parking is very limited, but the walk can be started at the Ibbeth Peril car park a mile (1½km) down the road, from where the route can be joined by crossing the footbridge and road on the south side of the river.

Lea Yeat is the little group of houses and cottages at the junction of the road to Dent station, known as the Coal Road. The cottage adjoining the bridge was built in 1701 as a Quaker meeting house. David Boulton tells us it was founded by Richard Harrison who, in his youth, was 'convinced' by George Fox, was repeatedly imprisoned and fined over the years, and in the end was driven to drink. There are records of the burials of 250 people in this cottage garden and under its concrete drive. The cottage below 'the Grange' was once Cowgill School, where each child had to bring 6d a year 'for coals'.

Start by walking along the road in the up-valley direction, for which there is no alternative, but it is no hardship because this is one of the pleasantest stretches of tarmac in the Dales. The young River Dee accompanies you on its bed of cobbles and limestone, the big slabs of rock enhancing the scene; in the pools there are some good-sized trout.

Listen, in spring, for woodland birds and practise your knowledge of the flowers that adorn the verges. Both pied and spotted flycatchers breed along the wooded beck. You may see the pied flycatcher near Lea Yeat or, in May, hear the male singing its insistent, up-and-down song as it establishes a territory and waits for its mate to arrive. Dippers and

pied wagtails frequent the river, while housemartins and swallows like the old farms. Among other flowers on the verges, varieties of cranesbill stand out: meadow cranesbill, wood cranesbill, shining cranesbill and herb robert. They all have five petals and are so named because each brown seed pod has a long beak.

Pass Harbourgill, built by the Quaker William Thistlethwaite in 1700 – his initials are over the door – and then the Sportsmans Inn. Before the inn was built (about 1790), beer was served in the nearby Cow Dub farmhouse. Over the bridge is Stonehouse where, in 1652, George Fox persuaded Thomas and George Mason to join the Quakers, and William Mason built a meeting house.

Stonehouse is at the foot of Arten Gill, which comes steeply down off the shoulder of Great Knoutberry Hill and under the arches of the railway viaduct. High Mill and Low Mill once used water power for spinning, then became factories for the cutting and polishing of 'Dent marble'. High Mill originally had a sixty foot (18m) waterwheel and Low Mill possessed a water-powered saw for cutting limestone. Remains of Low Mill are still visible just above the road.

Continue up the road past a limekiln and, beyond Scow Cottage, a pretty waterfall. The

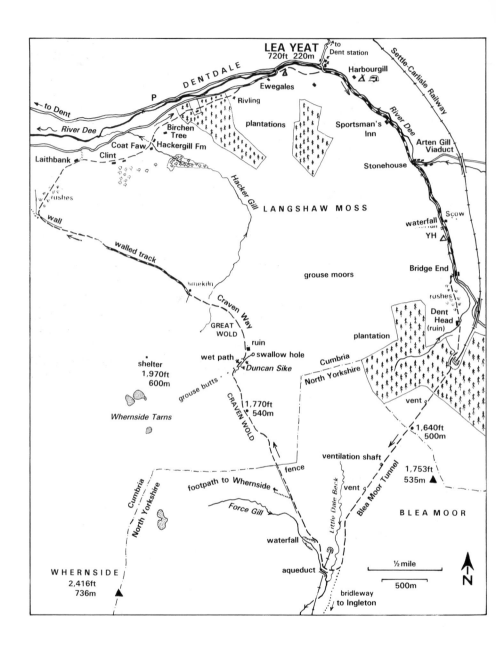

The eighteenth century Sportsmans Inn, and the dry riverbed of the River Dee near its junction with Arten Gill.

Great Scar limestone changes to the alternating beds of Yoredales which include sandstones and shales as well as limestones. Pass the attractively-sited youth hostel and then turn off opposite Bridge End Cottage, the home of Little Oak furniture. Go over the packhorse bridge – the sign says 'Blea Moor 2' – and over a rush-filled pasture to the derelict farmhouse of Dent Head, 1,000 feet (305m) above sea level. Beyond the farmyard, follow the beck and its waterfalls up to the railway, where grassed-over spoil heaps are a reminder of the excavation of Blea Moor tunnel. According to the season, the tunnel exit is decorated with colourful primroses, broom or heather, and beyond is a conifer plantation. There is a good view back along the railway line to the Dent Head viaduct.

Blea Moor is the most famous tunnel on the Settle to Carlisle line. It is one and a half miles (2.4km) long, took over four years to build and cost £120,000 in the 1870s, with 300 men employed in its construction. In their book *Settle to Carlisle*, Bill Mitchell and David Joy tell of the folk-hero miners who worked by candlelight and drilled holes for the dynamite while well-groomed tunnel horses, bedecked with ribbons, were used to remove the waste rock. In spite of all the difficulties less than a dozen serious accidents are recorded.

The walk follows the line of the tunnel.

Looking back to Dent Head viaduct and upper Dentdale from the ventilation shaft of Blea Moor Tunnel.

Climb steeply up through the plantation of larch and spruce, out onto the open moor, where there is a ventilation shaft and another on the crest of the fell. The shafts are brick-lined tubes which, in the construction of the tunnel, were used to bring rock debris to the surface. There were seven stationary steam-engines in use on Blea Moor working tram-ways, hauling up stone and sending men and supplies down. The footpath follows one of the longer tramlines. At the highest point, 1,640 feet (500m) above sea level, you pass from Cumbria into North Yorkshire.

It is an easy downhill walk to the third ventilation shaft, with only larks, meadow

pipits and wheatears to break the silence of the fells. The view ahead is of Ingleborough and Whernside, and a landscape around Ribble Head scattered with the rounded glacial hills of drumlins. Half a mile (800m) after passing the last vent, drop down from the track to cross Little Dale Beck and a bridge over the railway, 275 yards (250m) below the tunnel entrance. Alongside the bridge, the waters of Force Gill run in a magnificent stone aqueduct.

The walk now joins the Craven Old Way, a very old packhorse route from Dent to Ingleton along which coal, wool and other farm goods were carried. It is now part of a long-distance footpath – the Craven Way. The sign says 'Dentdale 4', and the path climbs up the right side of Force Gill which contains a fine waterfall. 'Force Gill' are two Norse words meaning waterfall ravine. When the beck is full the forty foot (12m) fall is an impressive sight.

The footpath here is part of the Three Peaks route, and there has been a lot of wear of the soft peaty ground. The addition of a boardwalk has proved successful in combating erosion. The Whernside path branches off to the left but this walk continues along the fence to the stile at the top, the county boundary again – where you are back in Cumbria. The whaleback of Whernside is prominent to the left.

On reaching limestone, the path becomes drier and walking is easier on the short green turf. The highest part, an altitude of 1,770 feet (540m), is along Craven Wold where better pastures mean more grazing sheep, so flowering plants have less chance.

Except for a short boggy stretch along Duncan Syke, the next mile (1½km) of the Craven Old Way is pleasant walking, where it follows a limestone shelf in otherwise very rough terrain. At a line of wooden shooting butts, turn down Duncan Syke to the ruin.

The view ahead is of Great Knoutberry Hill and Arten Gill viaduct. To the right of the ruin at Duncan Foot, the little stream disappears into a sink hole next to a cave.

The path curves to the left, before the ruin, and continues along a grass-covered limestone pavement dotted with violets. You may hear the plaintive call of the golden plover along here, and on the horizon to the left is a view of a shelter and cairn on the shoulder of Whernside. On reaching the intake wall, enter the greenest of green roads. There is a limekiln in good condition on the right, ahead are fine views of lower Dentdale and, further down the track, of Deepdale.

At the ladder stile signed 'Laithbank' go over the sloping rush-covered hillside, descend to some hummocky ground and over three more ladder stiles to the old farmhouse of Laithbank. Halfway down the drive, turn off round a barn to continue up to Clint and on to Coat Faw, then pass in front of the old farmhouse of Hackergill. Here the stile is overshadowed by a large bird-cherry tree and, after crossing a meadow, the path passes through the tall, damp conifers of Little Town plantation. After Rivling, reach the tarred lane and, just before Ewegales Bridge, take the path along the river back to Lea Yeat.

WALK 9: GRISEDALE FROM GARSDALE HEAD

Start:	Garsdale station. Grid Ref: 788 918
Distance:	5½ miles (9km)
OS Maps:	Pathfinder 617 or Landranger 98
Walking Time:	3 hours

This is a walk into the past, into a wild and well-hidden dale. Never below 1,000 feet (305m) above sea level, the 'dale that died' is at its best in the sunshine. It is full of interest and, since the walk begins at Garsdale Head, use can be made of trains on the Settle-Carlisle line. There is limited parking along the roadside below the station.

The green oasis of Grisedale, sheltered from westerly winds by the rounded mass of Baugh Fell and protected from the north by the bulk of Wild Boar Fell, is the most secluded and isolated of all the Dales. Measuring only two miles by half a mile (3 x 1km), it is situated high up near the watershed of England, where Grisedale Beck, which looks as though it ought to flow into Wensleydale, plunges into a gorge, turns sharply into Garsdale, and becomes the River Clough, later to join the Rawthey and the Lune. The dale is so well-hidden it cannot be seen from the nearby roads nor from the railway. Whichever way you enter the dale you must go over a hill before it comes into view.

The name Grisedale is Norse and means 'valley of young pigs', and traditionally the dale was the last sanctuary for wild boar in the Middle Ages. Other Viking place-names are Blake Mire (black bog), Scale (a *shieling* or summer pasture), How Shaw (hill copse, *shaw* being old English) and Mouse Syke (mouse stream).

In spite of its small size and lack of documented history, Grisedale has been a focus of attention. In 1975 Barry Cockroft made a television film and wrote a book about it, both entitled *The Dale that Died*, and in 1991 John Banks wrote *The Silent Stream*, a history of Grisedale which he called the 'little Quaker Dale'. Both tell, in different and

personal ways, the story of a once-thriving community which, in spite of a recent revival, left more ruined farmhouses than anywhere in the Dales.

Once known as Hawes Junction, Garsdale station, at over 1,100 feet (340m) above sea level, makes a good starting point for the walk. Before 1959, the engine of the train from Bradford to Hawes – known as 'Bonny-face' – was put on the famous turntable and travelled backwards into Wensleydale. The row of solidly-built cottages included the Temperance Hotel, with accommodation for commercial travellers.

From the station, go down the road and cross the A684 to a stile opposite, signed 'Flust 2'. Climb up for a view of the fine gorge and the waterfall of Clough Force. This winding ravine, cut by glacial meltwater at the end of the Ice Age, is the secret of Grisedale's seclusion, for it means there is no open view into the dale until you step into it.

Skirting the gorge high on the right, obtain your first sight of this broad and curving dale, and go on to the abandoned farmhouse of Blake Mire, a place which has been lived in continuously until the mid-twentieth century. Follow the signs, pass a barn and descend between the two barns of Rowantree, a homestead until the 1890s. Over to the left are Chapel House, the former Methodist chapel built in 1889, as a memorial to Methodist preacher Richard Atkinson, and

Garsdale station, looking to High Abbotside.

Beck House, once a barn. Both are now private dwellings.

The birds of Grisedale tend to be of the moorland variety: from early spring, lapwings perform their aerial acrobatics, skylarks add their unending song and meadow pipits, in their own song flight, with fluttering wings and tail held high, glide purposefully back to earth. On summer evenings, snipe carry on their 'drumming', when outer tail feathers vibrate as they slide through the air, and swallows swoop and dive to catch insects on the wing.

The way continues through fields, in May, golden with kingcups, to the whitewashed farmhouse of Moor Rigg. Up to the right,

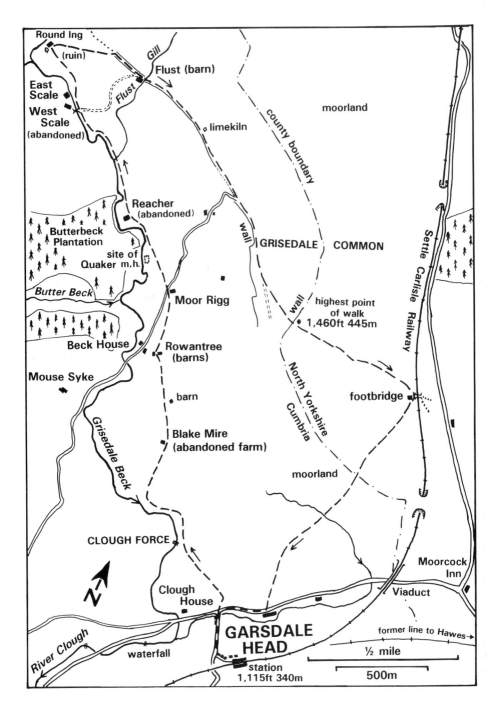

Round Ing
(ruin)
Flust Gill
Flust (barn)
East Scale
West Scale
(abandoned)
Flust
limekiln
county boundary
moorland
Reacher
(abandoned)
GRISEDALE COMMON
Butterbeck Plantation
site of Quaker m.h.
wall
Butter Beck
Moor Rigg
wall
highest point of walk
1,460ft 445m
Beck House
Rowantree
(barns)
Mouse Syke
Settle Carlisle Railway
barn
footbridge
Grisedale Beck
Blake Mire
(abandoned farm)
North Yorkshire
Cumbria
moorland
CLOUGH FORCE
Moorcock Inn
N
Clough House
Viaduct
GARSDALE HEAD
former line to Hawes →
River Clough
waterfall
station
1,115ft 340m
½ mile
500m

High Ing which once housed the Dame school is again in residence. Cross the road and in a damp patch, after kingcups and coltsfoot have withered, find feverfew, scabious, cow wheat, lesser stitchwort and meadowsweet.

Continue to the beck where, on the bank and now almost invisible, is the site of the Friends meeting house, said to have held eighty people. Built in 1706, it was attended for more than 150 years by most of the Grisedale families and several weddings were held there. By 1886 it was in bad repair and was being let to the Methodists. It was frequently flooded but an extra big flood is said to have reduced it to a pile of rubble, and the Methodists were allowed to take the stone to build their new chapel. This may have been the great flood of 1889 when a record 4½ inches (115mm) of rain fell in three hours. That August day Will Lund was out on the fells:

'I was sheltering under some rocks away the other side from Round Ing. On my own I was and I've never seen such rain. It was thundering too. Anyway, I just happened to look out further west to see if there was a break to it anywhere when I saw the ground beginning to rise up and about two or three hundred yards away from where I stood. Like a huge blister it was. Well I didn't know what to think. More and more ground rose until nearly three acres had come up to about four or five feet in height. And then it burst with a terrible noise, and a big wave came. A real torrent it was, carrying sods and rocks down into the valley.'

George Fox, founder of the Quakers, visited Grisedale in 1652 and it is probable that local Friends met first in their own homes, such as the Dawsons at Round Ing or the Harkers at Scale. Until 1689 the Quakers suffered for their faith. For preaching or holding meetings they had to pay fines, and many lost their possessions or were imprisoned in York gaol. Between 1655 and 1668, poor Thomas Winn's refusal to pay tithes or give money towards rebuilding the Garsdale chapel led on four occasions to the taking of his mare, some sheep, then a cow and four ewes, all of which were far more valuable than the small sums involved.

The abandoned farmhouse of Reacher (Reachey on the map) lies sheltered at the foot of Grisedale Pike, a shoulder of Baugh Fell where a group of stone cairns stand on the skyline. Behind the building is Butterbeck plantation which clothes the lower slopes of the fell. Follow the beck further upstream to a small stone bridge and two more empty farmhouses of East Scale and West Scale. All three of these farms were deserted round the turn of the century. The Friends burial ground occupies a corner here at Scale, but in spite of 100 burials recorded in the registers, there are no headstones and no sign of its exact whereabouts.

From the bridge, turn up the steep bank – still on the right side of the beck – on to Round Ing, aiming for a sycamore and ash, the last trees in the dale. This ruined farmhouse, its desertion accentuated by one or two dead trees, is almost flattened, but was obviously once an extensive building. Here the walk takes a change of direction, doubling back and up to join the ancient route which comes in from Uldale and Kirkby Stephen on its way to Hawes. Flust is now just a large barn, but the ruins below it were once the home of the Thompsons.

Go through the two metal gates at Flust and follow the farm track high above the dale. On the left is a limekiln with a small limestone quarry above it. Pass the upper end of the tarred Grisedale road and, keeping the wall on the right, follow the good path across the limetone plateau with a surface of grass-covered pavements. The ladder stile seen on the horizon is on the route. Here is the Main

The ruin of West Scale farmhouse, Grisedale; nearby is the former Quaker burial ground, although there are now no indications as to its exact whereabouts.

limestone, one of the larger outcrops in the Grisedale area where most of the limestone is covered by boulder clay. There are good views to Ingleborough, Whernside and Middleton Fell, with Baugh Fell and its group of stone men, marking Grisedale Pike, closer by.

Where the wall steps back to the right for a second time, turn from the worn path, off to the left, and aim for the ladder stile over a high stone wall which marks the county boundary. From the stile, look down from Cumbria into Yorkshire and a fine view of Wensleydale where stepped scarps face each other across the dale. Aiming for the left of these scarps, pass a broken-down wall of a sheep enclosure and make for the railway footbridge which crosses the Settle-Carlisle line below. Trains run regularly each day, but on a Saturday afternoon in summer you may be lucky and see one pulled by a steam engine on its way north.

On the way down through the rushes, marsh thistles and the moss *Polytrichum*, you may see one or two snipe. The most outstanding feature of this bird is its enormous bill which accounts for a quarter of its ten inch (25cm) length. The tip of the bill is flexible and very sensitive, most suitable for probing in damp mud for worms and other juicy morsels.

At the footbridge, and still on the nearside of the railway, pass in front of the white house and take the path up the hillside to the left of some old mine workings. To the left are the twelve arches of Dandrymire Viaduct. Curve slightly to the right to a ladder stile, where the path then goes over two rush-strewn hillocks and descends to the road by a line of cottages. Turn right down the road then left to reach Garsdale Station.

WALK 10: GARSDALE – VILLAGE AND DALE

Start: Longstone Common car park. Grid Ref: 694 912
Distance: 8 miles (13km)
OS Maps: Outdoor Leisure 2 or Landranger 98
Walking Time: 4 hours

This walk explores the peaceful valley of Garsdale. It starts from the viewpoint on Longstone Common, goes up the north side of the valley, passing several historic farmhouses, to Garsdale village. Then it returns along the banks of the River Clough. The walk can be shortened by two miles (3km) by turning back at Aye Gill. Longstone Common car park is on the A684 Sedbergh to Hawes road, two miles (3.5km) from Sedbergh where the unfenced road rises to a high point.

Of the four river valleys that converge near Sedbergh, Garsdale is perhaps the least known. Motorists from Hawes tend to pass through without stopping, cyclists enjoy the downhill run and walkers shun the area because the footpaths appear to be haphazard and disconnected. The dale hasn't the fame of Dentdale or the broad aspects of the Lune Valley. However, do not be deceived; Garsdale is a beautiful dale with many interesting attractions. Its deep, winding shape is flanked to the north by the bulky form of Baugh Fell, with Rise Hill on the south side, separating it from Dentdale. This peaceful valley sports patches of woodland, tree-lined gills and historic farmhouses with attractive names.

At the peak of Methodism, Garsdale had six Methodist chapels, from Grisedale to Frostrow chapel. The valley is also noted for its ghosts and tellings of strange noises, sudden winds, terrified beasts and shadowy figures.

In the summer of 1889, Garsdale was the scene of an extraordinary flood when, higher up the valley in Grisedale, four and a half inches (115mm) of rain fell in three hours, swelling the River Clough into a torrent. Three of the seven county bridges were completely wrecked, with the rest damaged, sections of road were washed away, all the footbridges and miles of walls and fences carried away, trees uprooted and houses filled

with sand and mud. The dale now has a good collection of substantial stone bridges, built to withstand future floods.

Perhaps the ideal way of seeing the dale is to leave the train at Garsdale Head and walk the ten miles (16km) or so to Sedbergh, from where there is a bus back to the station in the late afternoon to meet the southbound train.

This walk begins at Longstone Common car park, from which there are magnificent views of the Howgill Fells. Go down the narrow byroad to Danny Bridge. On the right the hummocky ground marks where limestone has been quarried for lime-making, the nearest outcrop of this useful rock to farmland further west. There is a fine limekiln just above Danny Bridge. The stone bridge straddles the beginning of a picturesque limestone gorge, along which runs the Sedgwick geology trail and where the River Clough – hardly big enough to be called a river – rushes on its way to join the Rawthey. Overlooking this lovely spot is a bank of yellow gorse and young trees, which make good cover for many woodland birds. Near to Danny Bridge is Garsdale Foot where James Inman was born, a man responsible for improvements in shipbuilding and navigation. He became Principal of the Royal Naval College, Portsmouth.

The sparrowhawk, green woodpecker and little owl all now breed in Garsdale, so it is

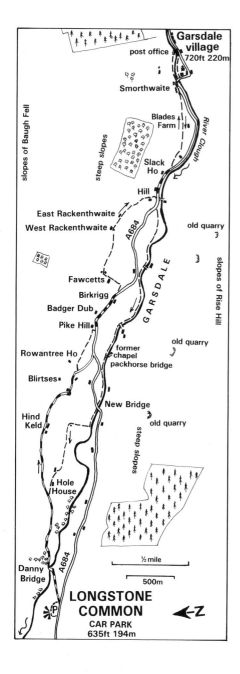

worth keeping a look out for them. The little owl is the smallest of the three, being only 8½ inches (22cm) in length. It is dusky brown streaked with white and has a fast, undulating flight. The green woodpecker is bigger – 12½ inches (32cm) – dull green with a yellow rump and also has a bounding flight, closing its wings every three or four beats, then sweeping up into a tree. The male sparrowhawk measures only 11 inches (28cm), the female being noticeably larger. They have short, broad wings, and dashing bursts of rapid wing-beats are followed by a short glide as they chase their prey over the hedges or through the trees.

Continue up the narrow road, bordered with horsetails, ferns and blackberries, past Hole House Farm – the return route comes in here – and on to Hind Keld, about a mile (1.5km) along the lane. Here is a traditional farmhouse with a fine corbelled chimney. Stone supports allow the chimney to jut out on the upper storey, continuing the line of a stone hood over the main fireplace. This narrow gated road is little used by traffic and, in places, even has grass growing down the centre. But from it there are fine views along the dale.

After passing the whitewashed cottage of Lindsey Fold and then a dip in the road, turn off on a track to the left – signed 'Pike Hill' – leading to an isolated cottage called Blirtses. Before reaching the cottage, turn off the track along a wall and along to Pike Hill Cottage and the A684.

Turn left along the road past Badger Dub, an old farmhouse at the foot of a small plantation with a fine monkey puzzle tree. James Haygarth lived at Badger Dub from 1818 to 1834, and kept a fascinating country diary in which he noted the first snow of the winter, the date when crows began to build their nests, and when he heard the first cuckoo and saw his first swallow. He also names many people of the dale, those who were married and those who died. The diary

74

– transcribed by Kevin Lancaster in the *Sedbergh Historian* – also records James Haygarth as being the local dentist, extracting teeth for those in need.

A quarter of a mile (400m) along, pass Birk Rigg which, in 1610, was the scene of crime. On the death of the widow owner, several men from Wensleydale forcefully took over the house and kidnapped the nine year old daughter.

Leave the road, left, at the sign for a caravan site. From here there are extensive views up the dale. The greatest area of meadowland and good pasture is on this northern, sunny side of the valley, where most of the farms are situated. The shady southern slopes make poor farmland and are covered in rushes low into the valley, where once it was more intensively farmed. There are many groups of trees along the dale, including some tall pines, and lines of woodland pick out the side gills.

Follow the lane up past Fawcetts Farm (signed 'Hill'), through a very long metal gate, and turn right in front of a barn. The path leads through the fields to West Rackenthwaite. Go through the farmyard and past the front door of the farmhouse to East Rackenthwaite, where once lived James Nelson who, in 1620, purchased from Lord

The three-storey cottage of Hind Keld, and Garsdale Pike.

The delicate flowers of pink purslane are not a common sight, but grow profusely along the banks of the River Clough.

Scrope one fifth of the manor of Garsdale. The farm is the site of a grange of Coverham Abbey in Wensleydale.

Go along and down through the fields to the left of Hill Farm and the road again at Aye Gill. (For a shorter walk return down the river from here.)

Continue up the valley, passing Slack Cottage and Slack House Farm where the river flows alongside the road, then take the footpath to the left signed 'to Smorthwaite'. After a group of cottages, go along the road for a few strides and continue up the left side of the river for another 330 yards (300m). After a metal gate, go down and round the back of the post office to the footbridge and road. The post office is a general store for the village of Garsdale and an information point for the National Park. Houses and cottages are strung out along the 'street'. There is a church, school, two Methodist chapels and a garage. The church was rebuilt in 1861, although back in the thirteenth century there was a church here under the care of the canons of Easby Abbey at Richmond. The school was founded in 1634 by Thomas

Dawson and Garsdale Hall, on the corner, was once an inn. It is said that the beer brewed for this public house was extra strong and that only a Garsdale man could take a pint and still walk straight.

A mile higher up the valley is the farmhouse of Raygill, birthplace in 1734 of the mathematician, John Dawson. As a youngster, minding his father's sheep, he worked out a complex mathematical formula for conic sections while sitting on a rock high above Raygill, now known as Dawsons Rock. Later, Dawson became a surgeon in Sedbergh, where Cambridge mathematics students came to receive his coaching.

From the post office, cross the bridge and go first down the left bank of the river, then return along the same route through fields to Aye Gill Bridge. Eighty yards (70m) beyond Aye Gill, turn off (signed 'New Bridge') for a lovely river walk down the dale. Grey wagtail, heron and mallard are all to be seen along the wooded river, where butterbur, bistort and pink purslane grow in abundance on the banks. Pebbles in the river show 'imbrication' where the flattish slabs all slope upstream as a result of the current. From 'fossil' examples in rocks, ancient current directions can be determined. Finds of North Sea oil depend on such detective work.

The house on the road is Swarthgill House, a three storey, whitewashed farmhouse in which the upper windows have been blocked out. This was the birthplace of John Haygarth, contemporary of John Dawson, who went to Cambridge and became a famous surgeon in Leeds. Haygarth was a pioneer of isolating patients in the treatment of infectious diseases, and John Dawson used his methods in preventing an outbreak of smallpox in Sedbergh in 1780. Keep along the right bank to a tiny Wesleyan Methodist chapel, dated 1863, on the opposite bank, and a packhorse bridge.

At New Bridge, cross the road and continue a little further along the riverbank, turning away and following the signs for Hole House. On the way is a view of Hind Keld, also a three storey cottage on the hillside above. Climbing gradually, the path weaves below Stephens Farm and above Hole House to emerge on the little byroad on which the walk started. Descend to Danny Bridge and up the other side to the car park.

WALK 11: RIVER WALK AND THE SEDGWICK TRAIL

Start: Sedbergh. Grid Ref: 657 921
Distance: 7 miles (11km)
OS Maps: Outdoor Leisure Map 2 (or Pathfinder 617), OS Touring Map & Guide 6
Walking Time: 4 hours

Enjoy some wonderful riverside walking in this lowland circuit, first along the Rawthey Valley and then into lower Garsdale, with some good bird-watching. In one short, very scenic stretch of the River Clough, the Sedgwick Trail provides a superb demonstration of the geology of the area, especially of the Dent Fault. Take time to appreciate the story in the rocks, and return to Sedbergh via attractive farmhouses and striking views of the Howgill Fells. An informative leaflet on the Sedgwick Trail can be obtained from the National Park centre in Sedbergh.

Sedbergh is Old Norse for flat-topped hill. The Normans built a motte and bailey castle on Castle Haw which might have been the original hill. They also built a fine church, which still retains some Norman stonework. The market charter came in the thirteenth century and Wednesday market day is still the busiest day of the week. The famous school was founded in 1525 by Dr Roger Lupton, a local man who became canon of Windsor and provost of Eton. It was a chantry school – on land granted by Coverham Abbey – endowed with six scholarships to St Johns College, Cambridge. After a chequered history it was rebuilt in 1716, a building which now houses the school's old library collection and faces the Dent road next to the car park. Its former pupils include Francis Howgill, Quaker, Anthony Fothergill, physician, John Dawson, mathematician, John Haygarth, physician, James Inman, nautical scientist, and Adam Sedgwick, geologist.

By the 1760s roads converging on Sedbergh were made turnpikes to take coaches such as the 'Lord Exmouth' from Lancaster to Newcastle. The knitting industry was strong and, with the introduction of machinery, expanded with the building of Hebblethwaite Hall mill in 1792 and its successor at Farfield in 1837. The story of the knitters and these two mills is told in Marie Hartley and

Joan Ingilby's *The Old Hand-knitters of the Dales*. Unlike many Dales villages and towns, Sedbergh has increased its population steadily over the last 200 years and it still has a bright future – as a tourist centre, especially for walkers.

Beginning near the parish church, go along the cobbled Main Street, past the National Park information centre, to the east end of the town. Turn right, across Back Lane, to take the path alongside the playing fields and over the hill past the school. Keep straight on and down towards the river. A stile takes you by a mill-race decked in spring with kingcups and wild garlic, and in summer by masses of the tall Himalayan balsam or policeman's helmet. At a small stone bridge, join the built-up bank of the River Rawthey.

Just opposite a footbridge – where the mill-race leaves the river – is a low sandy rivercliff, the home to dozens of sand martins. Their welcome arrival in late March marks the end of winter, and their harsh twittering as they wheel about over the river can be heard throughout the summer. Other birds along this stretch are the goosander, common sandpiper and, on the gravel banks, the oystercatcher.

Pass the two stone arches of New Bridge and continue along the riverbank, with Baugh Fell ahead and the rounded peaks of Crook,

Sickers and Knott to the left. Beyond a large pebble bank and just before Straight Bridge you get a view through the trees of the River Clough which, having descended the length of Garsdale, here enters and swells the Rawthey. But its entrance is rather an awkward one. The Rawthey is lower than the Clough, which has to descend by a waterfall to reach the right level. Also, instead of the tributary gliding in at the normal sharp angle, it enters head-on at right angles.

From April, the handsome pied flycatcher proclaims its territory along the river. It nests in tree holes and its plump, boldly-pied form may be seen as it darts for insects and flicks its wings and tail. You may also see the fly-catching antics of its cousin, the more soberly-coloured spotted flycatcher. Either of these summer visitors is a delight to watch.

At Straight Bridge, a glance over the parapet reveals an outcrop of unusual rock in the riverbed, made up of large red-stained pebbles like some giant concrete, here seen at its coarsest with boulders up to two feet (60cm) across. This is the Garsdale conglomerate, a bed of rock seen here and there from Shap Wells to Kirkby Lonsdale. The presence of red iron oxides denote a desert environment and its age is early Carboniferous (350 million years old). The rock provided the Rawthey with its name which means 'red river'.

Go over the bridge, and immediately along a very narrow hedge-lined lane to Garsdale Bridge and the banks of the River Clough. Continue up the left side of the river – on the other side is Farfield Mill – where rocky outcrops of grey Silurian flags and grits occupy the streambed, forming a series of natural weirs one after the other. One of these shelves of rock was once used as a weir to channel off water to the mill. One of the attractions of the river is the way it rushes over its rocky bed. Farfield Mill, run by the Dovers, once made horse blankets, supplying the royal family. It changed hands in 1937,

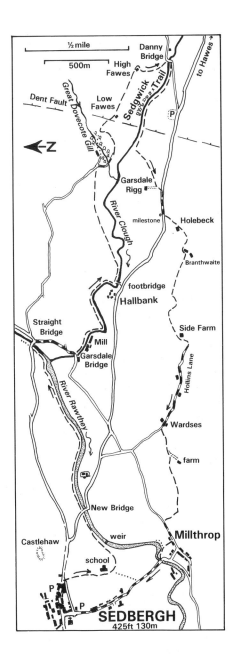

but is now again producing woollen goods as Pennine Tweeds.

The tree-lined bank of alder, elm, sycamore and hazel offers cover for many woodland birds, including the treecreeper; the bright, high-pitched song of the wren accompanies you all the way. The river is frequented by dippers, and pied and grey wagtails. In the early spring the grey wagtail's sulphur-yellow front and rear are sparklingly bright and, on open fields, flocks of fieldfare and mistle thrush feed.

Go past the footbridge – which leads to the main road and the hamlet of Hallbank – and climb away from the river to obtain a view through the trees into the S-shaped gorge. To the rear, Hallbank stands out on its hilltop, once the homes of workers in the early mill. The bank ahead is scattered with yellow gorse. Follow the series of stiles and a double fence to reach Dowbiggin Lane.

Turn right – signed Danny Bridge – along the lane and, in the spring, among the primroses, wood sorrel and wild strawberry, look for the dainty little blooms of moschatel. The cubic arrangement on each stem of four greenish flowers, each facing a different direction, with an upward-facing one on the top, has led to the attractive name of townhall clock. It is such an unusual plant that, until recent discoveries of two relatives in China, it stood all alone in its own botanical family.

Cross the wooded Great Dovecote Gill. A steep bank on the right is covered with the mountain (or lemon-scented) fern, a bright and attractive yellow-green when young. Go up through the metal gate and curve round to the left to another metal gate, then along a wall to High Fawes. Cross a wooden stile, round the farmhouse, to a double stile at the bottom left corner of a field, bringing you out at the bottom of the hill to Danny Bridge.

There is a fine view up Garsdale from the stoney, gorse-covered slopes. The thick piles of stones are clearance cairns, created by laborious clearing of the land of its rocks and

stones to improve the grazing. Just above the bridge is a limekiln, a clue that you are now on limestone and east of the Dent Fault. Just below the bridge on the other side is Danny Cave where, legend has it, a farmer sent his dog which, after a few days, emerged in Dentdale without its hair!

The Sedgwick Trail begins at Danny Bridge. It was opened in 1985, in recognition, 200 years earlier, of the birth in Dent of Adam Sedgwick, the great dalesman and Cambridge professor of geology. This attractive gorge with its deep pools and limestone riverbed is the prettiest part of Garsdale. There are wooded slopes on the right, rocky outcrops on the left and the gurgling River Clough below – a beautiful place in spring sunshine.

Between points one and nine – marked by wooden posts – there is a continuous exposure of Great Scar limestone of Carboniferous age (340 million years ago) showing some interesting features, including one or two bands of shale and sandstone. Near the bridge the limestone beds slope steeply upstream and, at point five, they show folding – a distinct upfold or anticline being visible in the far bank. At Tom Croft Cave (point seven) the strata have been pushed into a vertical position, and a little further on are actually overturned. Point nine shows the dramatic outcrop of limestone smashed to fragments by the fault movement and forming a breccia – angular pieces of rock cemented together – full of mineral veins.

The gorge and the limestone comes to an end, and at point ten the Brathay Flags – of Silurian age (425 million years old) – dip downstream. Between the two exposures is the Dent Fault along which, at the end of Carboniferous time, the Lake District rocks rose up as much as 8,000 feet (2.5km) above those of the Pennines. It was the pressure along the fault which produced the sharp folding in the limestone. Adam Sedgwick was the first to discover the fault and to interpret

The spotted flycatcher is outstanding to watch: it perches upright on a branch and, exercising its long wings, dives for flies and regains the same perch time after time.

its importance as a major feature of the earth's crust. In spite of great advances in earth science, his interpretation still stands today.

The change at the fault from limestone to flagstone is marked by an abrupt change in vegetation on the bank above, from short green turf with wild thyme, to coarse grasses and rushes with heather and sphagnum.

On top of the Brathay Flags there is a reddish pebble-bed, the Garsdale conglomerate – also seen at point eleven – which is about 60 million years younger than the flags

beneath it. The surface separating the two is known as an unconformity. In the National Park leaflet, Dr Rickards suggests that the red conglomerate fills a hollow in the flagstone which could have been gravels on the floor of a desert wadi (or gorge). Fossil graptolites, looking rather like small bits of fretsaw blade, occur in the Brathay Flags, helping to date them. They were floating marine organisms, the skeletons of which are found in former oceanic muds.

Continue for 100 yards (90m) or so to pick up an old sunken packhorse track from the

The River Clough along the Sedgwick Trail, a beautiful stetch of Garsdale.

river, and follow the wall round to reach the road opposite the entrance to Garsdale Rigg Farm. In April you may see peacock butterflies which have become more common in recent years, perhaps due to the mild winters. These insects have hibernated over winter. They lay their eggs on nettle leaves, on which you may see the hairy black caterpillars feeding in July, and the beautiful new butterflies emerge in the autumn.

Turn right along the road for 300 yards (275m) to the metal-faced milestone ('Sedbergh 2'), left through Holebeck and its gates up to a ladder stile, then a gate gap to the pretty white-painted farm of Low Branthwaite. Skirting the farmhouse on the lower side, take the stiles opposite the front door and head for a large barn. There are tremendous views of the Howgills from this path – enchanting scenery, especially when there

is a dusting of snow on the tops. Following the field boundary, go round the left side of the barn and follow tractor tracks to Side Farm, passing between the buildings to enter Hollins Lane.

This lovely winding lane connects attractive farmhouses and cottages, but, after passing the whitewashed Wardses Cottage, turn left off the road onto a farm track. Then where this track turns up to the left, keep straight forward to a stile at the wall corner. Keep on through a gate gap and stiles which eventually lead down to the road; turn left to approach Millthrop. After the first row of cottages, go between the houses to the River Rawthey where rocks and shingle in the river make a delightful scene, a good place for a stop or a picnic. Go over the bridge and up the road back to Sedbergh.

WALK 12: ULDALE AND WANDALE FROM RAWTHEY BRIDGE

Start: Rawthey Bridge. Grid Ref: 713 988
Distance: 9 miles (14½km)
OS Maps: Pathfinder 617 or Landranger 98
Walking Time: 4½ hours

Starting from Rawthey Bridge, this walk explores two little-known dales. It penetrates the upper reaches of the River Rawthey to visit some delightful waterfalls, then crosses back into isolated Wandale and along a fine mid-level track between the historic farmhouse of Adamthwaite and the hamlet of Narthwaite. There is parking by the A683 just below Rawthey Bridge which lies about a mile (1.6km) north of Cross Keys Hotel on the Sedbergh to Kirkby Stephen road.

The road from Sedbergh was improved as a turnpike in 1765 as far as Rawthey Bridge. In those days there was a stone circle near the bridge, but, in 1824, when the bridge was rebuilt and a new section of road constructed to the north, the stones from the circle were incorporated in the foundations. The high, stone arch has been built to last and, below the parapets, the bridge is decorated with a carved stone head on one side and a gargoyle on the other.

The Lancaster to Newcastle stage coach made use of the new road and, one cold winter's night, the curate from Sedbergh and a gentleman and lady were travelling in the coach to Kirkby Stephen. When it reached the Cross Keys at Cautley, the driver dropped off for some hot refreshment, but the horses suddenly set off at a trot. The landlord gave chase but failed to catch them; then the curate, aware of the situation, climbed out onto the step, but slipped and fell onto the ice. The runaway coach rattled on over Rawthey Bridge, the two other passengers quite unaware that they had no driver. The curate managed to walk to the next inn where he borrowed a horse and, expecting to see the coach overturned in a ditch, arrived in Kirkby Stephen to find it patiently waiting outside the Kings Arms, the next scheduled stop, and the passengers quite unaware of their adventure.

Starting from the road just below Rawthey Bridge – next to the National Park sign – follow the wheeled track as it winds high over Bluecaster Side. This is the pre-1765 road from Sedbergh to Rawthey Bridge, and the path up Uldale turns off to the left before a stream crossing to regain a view of the river half a mile (800m) further on. Uldale means wolf valley.

The route crosses the Dent Fault and on to the limestone, denoted by a line of shakeholes. A little further, limestone strata are steeply tilted where they have been upturned by the force of the fault movement. After a limekiln on the right, the path goes closer to the river where scattered woodland adds charm to the dale. The colours of the birches, beeches, rowan and hawthorn are resplendent in the autumn. Where the track branches down to a footbridge, descend to see a fine view of the first waterfalls of Uldale. There are five steps to the series of falls above the bridge, and one below, all in the limestone.

Staying on the right bank, the path clings to the side of the ravine, giving rough walking in places but a good vantage point. Two more single drop falls are encountered before

The view up Uldale – meaning 'wolf valley' – from the ruin of Wandale Farm.

reaching Rawthey Gill Quarry, where sandstone for building and flagstone for roofing have been quarried, the strata being horizontal again. In among the rocks grows the little plant New Zealand willowherb, its bare brown stems topped by tiny white flowers, making it quite different from other flowers. Wild thyme, foxglove and heath speedwell are also common here.

Walk through the length of the old quarry as far as Whin Stone Gill, a tributary waterfall on the opposite bank. This is the crossing place with a change of direction down the far bank. (If the river is in spate, retreat to the footbridge at the lower falls.)

Before crossing the Rawthey, continue upstream for another 200 yards (180m) to see two more waterfalls, the higher one of which can be spectacular when the the river is full.

From just below Whin Stone Gill on the right bank, a good track climbs up to Blea Gill Bridge where there is a small stone bridge. Pass Uldale House, dated 1828, and along the lane over Needlehouse Gill, another deep and wooded ravine with a more substantial stone bridge, then follow the unfenced road.

Not far from the Street there is a line of shakeholes by the roadside, marking the presence of limestone dissolved by the action of water. One of them is a swallow hole where a stream disappears into a cave. You may see a little owl in this area, a bird that is active during the day. It is only nine inches (23cm) long – the smallest British owl – and may be seen perching in a prominent place. Its swooping flight is like that of a woodpecker.

The Street is the old road to Kirkby Stephen before the 1825 turnpike was built.

84

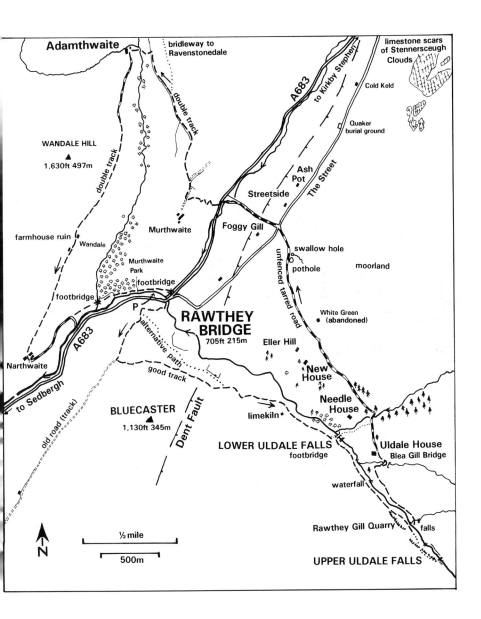

Higher up the road, at Doven Gill, is a Quaker burial ground, and up to the right are the limestone scars of Stennerskeugh Clouds. *Stennerskeugh* is Old Norse for 'stony track'.

Cross the Street and go through the gate, between two walls and down to a footbridge over Sally Beck. In May or June both the spotted flycatcher and garden warbler have nest sites nearby. There is plenty of cover for birds among the hawthorn, wild roses and blackthorn. The small brown-and-buff garden warbler, the size of a robin, has little to

85

The early-flowering primrose heralds the arrival of spring.

distinguish it, and when it sings it 'gabbles on' in long phrases. The spotted flycatcher is also a small brown bird, and is distinguished by its upright stance and habit of returning to its perch after darting for a fly. In the wet patch grow kingcups, marsh horsetail, cotton grass and marsh lousewort.

Cross the main road and zigzag up the steep hillside between two gullies to the small gate at the top, and on to the track which comes from the little community of Mur thwaite, the roofs of which are just visible Turn right along the track, forking left at the wall corner. The isolated valley of Wandale soon comes into view. On reaching the wall on the left, follow it down to a gate imme diately above Adamthwaite Farm, dropping down to a sturdy stone bridge over Wandale Beck. The old farm of Adamthwaite has the dated lintel 'TA 1684' above the door, and between the house and barn is an old spinning gallery. The farm is linked by a small road to the village of Ravenstonedale 2½ miles (4km) to the north.

Turn left to a walled green lane, to begin a lovely scenic track above Wandale with excellent views across to Uldale and the hill of Wild Boar Fell, Baugh Fell, Whernside and Middleton Fell. Buzzards patrol the skies, redstarts find cover in the trees and wheatears flit about the old walls and ruins By late autumn, the berries on the hawthorns attract fieldfares by the hundred.

Narthwaite is a group of farm buildings and cottages. A Quaker meeting room was made on the upper floor of a large barn, and meetings held from 1793 until 1907. The barn is distinguished by having alternating courses of limestone and sandstone.

From Narthwaite, go down the track, then through the gate on the bend into a field to a small bridge across Wandale Beck, continu ing along a field below the wood. At the far end of this ancient meadow grow yellow rattle, betony, smooth St Johns-wort, meadow vetchling and fragrant orchid. The orchid has a bright pink spike of sugar candy-flower smelling of carnations.

Cross into the equally ancient wood of birch, oak, rowan and hazel and up the beckside. Beyond the wood, scattered haw thorns stretch up the slopes; another small bridge, this time over Sally Beck, brings you onto the road and back to Rawthey Bridge.

WALK 13: CAUTLEY SPOUT AND THE CALF

Start: Sedbergh. Grid Ref: 658 921
Distance: 9½ miles (15km)
OS Maps: Pathfinder 617 or Landranger 98
Walking Time: 5 hours

The Calf is the highest point of the Howgill Fells at 2,220 feet (676m). This inspiring walk involves a five mile (8km) 'walk-in' through the old farms of Cautley, a very steep climb up the side of Cautley Spout, and a descent on a fine track over Brant Fell and Arant Haw to return down Settlebeck Gill. There are two good car parks in Sedbergh.

Sedbergh is a grand little town. Cheerful and friendly, it provides well for both residents and visitors. It has a National Park centre, a useful selection of shops, three pubs and a weekly market. Its secondhand book shop is second to none. It is perhaps best known for its public school and its Quaker connections (*see walk 14*). In Railtons Yard it still retains an old spinning gallery, a reminder of the days when yarn had to be supplied to the large number of hand knitters in the area.

The town has had a market since 1251, and its market cross and steps survived until about 1870; the stone ball from the top of the cross is now at Brigflatts Meeting House. The Wednesday market is still the busiest day of the week, though stalls have now moved from the narrow cobbled street to the nearby Joss Lane car park. The livestock auction has a site on the Kendal road and takes place on Fridays.

The parish church is at the centre of the town and, though it has work of several periods, it still retains some of its Norman origins. It was dedicated to St Andrew and a small statue of the saint stands in a niche above the porch. The church was largely restored in 1886.

To start the walk, go to the end of the cobbled Main Street and, after fifty yards (45m), turn left on a footpath that passes below Castlehaw Tower, the Norman motte and bailey which crowned this small wooded hill. The original wooden castle was built to guard the entrance to Garsdale and the route along the Rawthey Valley. There is a chance to visit the site near the end of this walk.

Cross the stream and go up a narrow lane on the path to Underbank. The view to the right is of Garsdale, until the path curves round to the left to strike up the side of the Rawthey Valley. Underbank is an old farmhouse and converted barn. Roger Moister was born here and in 1831 emigrated to Pennsylvania, where he became known as an ardent Methodist preacher. His son William was a missionary in Africa and the West Indies before returning to Sedbergh.

Go down the farm track then left through the fields, past a line of fine bird cherries, to cross Ashbeck Gill. The three rounded hills to the left are Crook, Sickers and Knott. Nearby, an archaeological dig revealed a medieval settlement, an area still known as Little Sedbergh. The fine building of Stone Hall, with its rounded, Westmorland-style chimneys and three-storey porch, is one of the oldest in the district, dating back to about 1600.

Continue in the same direction to Hollin Hall, a farmhouse built in 1711 by Edmund Bland. The humble barn shows lines of 'throughs' jutting out at intervals and vertical

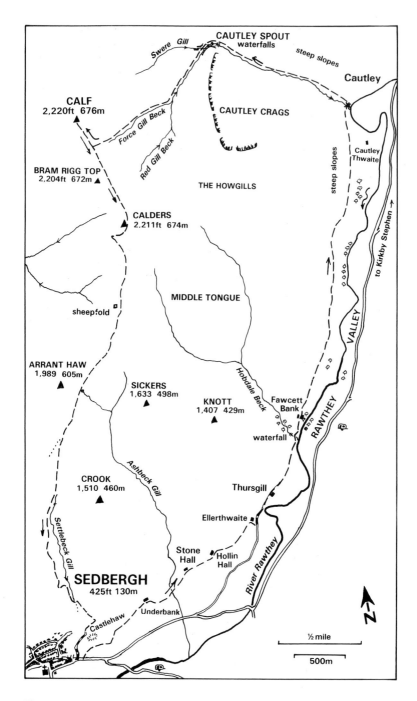

CAUTLEY SPOUT
waterfalls

Swere Gill

steep slopes

Cautley

CALF
2,220ft 676m

CAUTLEY CRAGS

Cautley
Thwaite

Force Gill Beck

Red Gill Beck

BRAM RIGG TOP
2,204ft 672m

THE HOWGILLS

steep slopes

CALDERS
2,211ft 674m

to Kirkby Stephen

MIDDLE TONGUE

sheepfold

Hobdale Beck

ARRANT HAW
1,989 605m

SICKERS
1,633 498m

KNOTT
1,407 429m

Fawcett
Bank

RAWTHEY VALLEY

waterfall

Ashbeck Gill

CROOK
1,510 460m

Thursgill

Ellerthwaite

Settlebeck Gill

River Rawthey

Stone
Hall

Hollin
Hall

SEDBERGH
425ft 130m

N

Castlehaw

Underbank

½ mile

500m

slits to air the hay, another example of Westmorland rural architecture. After passing through the farmyard, go straight across the next field to a ladder stile.

Pass the upper end of a stone wall and go down the near side of the white house (Ellerthwaite) to join a lane. Bird boxes erected in this valuable patch of oak wood here on the bank of the rushing river have attracted the pied flycatcher, a bird whose range and numbers have been extended by such provision.

From the cobbled yard of Thursgill, an excellent path – an old packhorse route to Cautley – continues on the lower slopes of the Howgills, and there are wonderful views up the valley and across to Baugh Fell. Cross Hobdale Beck – a place for hobgoblins where it plunges down beneath a stone bridge, from which you can see the River Rawthey as it flows noisily below in a deep wooded gorge. The path crosses several streams and springs where, in the rowan and hawthorns, you may see the coal tit, always restless as it flits from twig to twig. Turn up through a gate to continue above the intake wall, and descend to a footbridge over Cautley Holme Beck, where you get your first view of Cautley Spout.

Here is the most rugged scenery of the Howgills. The long, steep face of Cautley Crag stretches to the left of the falls. It was formed in the Ice Age, the backwall of a glacial corrie – the peak of the last glaciation being about 20,000 years ago. The great thickness of ice cut back into the mountain to form the steep rocky crag, grinding out a hollow below. The falls of Cautley Spout tumble 650 feet (200m) in a series of cataracts. After prolonged rain the Spout is so full of water it becomes one of the most spectacular falls in the country. On such a day in February 1992, Harry Griffin visited them and, in his *Country Diary*, said you could 'almost feel the fellside shaking and shuddering with the thuds of falling water'. Ahead are Yarlside screes, now stabilised by vegetation.

Take the track up towards the falls. Flowers in the well-grazed turf include the inconspicuous marsh cudweed, a weedy little plant with a silvery-grey coating of cotton-wool.

The base of the falls makes a good place for a picnic. From here, there follows a very steep but exciting climb to the top of the staircase of falls. In the deep ravine to the left, rowan and ash secure a foothold and, with the aid of binoculars, you may make out devilsbit scabious, golden rod and knapweed. A small wooden cross on the way up commemorates the life of Pauline Lord.

At the top of the steep climb, turn left to cross Swere Gill, follow Red Gill Beck for a third of a mile (550m), then take the right-hand valley along Force Gill Beck. Several small springs leak out of the fellside and in these wet places the sharp-eyed botanist will

The formation of a corrie, as at Cautley Crags.

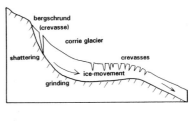

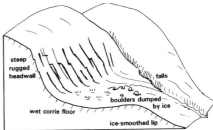

Water crowfoot has bright little flowers.

be delighted to see starry saxifrage, New Zealand willowherb and a tiny forget-me-not.

The beck becomes smaller as its source is reached, where it emerges from a spring, and the route brings you onto a broad saddle between the Calf and Bram Rigg. To the left is the way to Sedbergh but first turn right for a 330 yard (300m) diversion to visit the top of the Calf, the highest point on the Howgills. At 2,220 feet (676m) the views are panoramic, west to the Lakeland mountains, north to Cross Fell and Mickle Fell, east to Wild Boar and Great Shunner fells, and south to the Three Peaks and the Lune Valley.

Return to the saddle and continue straight on over Bram Rigg and Calders, both only a few feet lower than the Calf. Approaching the top of the latter – marked by a cairn – a fence

runs parallel to the footpath, down to Rowan-tree Grain. From near the sheepfold there is a fine view to the right of the interlocking spurs of a stream-eroded valley, in which Bram Rigg Beck makes its way to Chapel Beck and the Lune.

Skirt the left side of Arant Haw, with views of Baugh Fell, Rise Hill and Whernside, and pass Swere Gill Well (another Swere Gill), a small spring below the path where water crowfoot and golden saxifrage grow and, later in the year, lesser spearwort and forget-me-not.

Ahead are two cairned peaks, Crook on the left and Winder on the right. Soon, at a small cairn, fork left to descend by Settlebeck Gill between the two hills. The stream has cut a deep V-shaped notch in the landscape, with

The falls of Cautley Spout tumble 650 feet (200m) in a series of spectacular cataracts.

a pretty waterfall. Keep to the right of a spring-fed tributary for a pleasant, easy descent to the intake wall and an iron kissing-gate. Patches of gorse clothe the hillside, and the turf is generally so short that the sheep have taken to nibbling the young gorse shoots, giving the bushes a clipped appearance. Ahead you can see the mounds of Castlehaw and the district of Sedbergh known as Settle-beck.

Just before the stile, turn left through a gate and down a field to a tarred lane, to visit Castlehaw Tower, a motte and bailey, open to the public during daylight hours. A wooden castle was built on this strategic site by the Normans to defend the routes to the north and east. The mounds are well-preserved, steep and regular, where bluebells are later replaced by harebells. The lane brings you down to the top end of Main Street.

WALK 14: BRIGFLATTS AND FOX'S PULPIT

Start: Sedbergh. Grid Ref: 657 921
Distance: 8½ miles (13km)
OS Maps: Pathfinder 617 or Landranger 97
Walking Time: 4½ hours

Here is a pilgrimage which takes you to the very heart of the birthplace of Quakerism. From Sedbergh we first visit the charming old meeting house at Brigflatts, pass through the grounds of Ingmire Hall, then climb steeply up through Hawkrigg Wood onto Firbank Fell to Fox's Pulpit. Descend to the Lune and return via farmland and Howgill Lane. There are magnificent views of the Howgills and plenty of local Quaker history. Sedbergh has good car parks.

Sedbergh is known both for its public school and its Quaker connections. In 1525, Roger Lupton of Howgill – who became provost of Eton – was the founder of a small chantry school, where choir boys were taught Latin. Rebuilt in 1716, the fine building of the old grammar school on Finkle Street now houses a library and museum. Extensive Victorian buildings and playing fields now cover a large area on the southern edge of the town, and the school is one of the most famous in the north of England. Among its eminent masters was John Dawson of Garsdale who became a celebrated mathematician in Cambridge – there is a commemorative bust of him in the church; and among its pupils was the pioneer geologist Adam Sedgwick.

On Wednesday the 9th June 1652, George Fox preached for several hours in Sedbergh churchyard to a large crowd who had come to the Whitsun fair. A captain asked why he didn't preach in the church, to which Fox replied that the church was not a building but a fellowship of people. He had many supporters, one of whom was Francis Howgill who declared Fox 'speaks with authority'. The following Sunday, George Fox went to Firbank Fell and spoke to a thousand people.

It was a time of unrest. Charles I had been beheaded and there was such confusion in the established Church that many people

such as the Seekers of the north of England looked for a more meaningful way forward, and these were the people who flocked to hear George Fox. The events in Sedbergh mark the beginning of Quakerism and the Society of Friends.

Start the walk by taking the path below the church and left, round the cricket field. Keep straight on, through all the kissing gates, crossing the road and approaching the River Rawthey, to the hamlet of Birks. Turn left at the road and then follow the footpath sign through the fields to Brigflatts. Just before crossing the line of the old railway, you will see Borrett Farm on the right. This was where Justice Benson and his wife lived, and where the first meeting of the Seekers took place with George Fox, a few days before he entered Sedbergh. The Bensons were loyal supporters of Fox but suffered greatly for their faith. Their son, for example, was born in York prison.

Pass under the disused railway. Closed in 1953, this was the line from Ingleton to Tebay of the old London North Western Railway, which once competed with the Settle-Carlisle line.

Continue to the hamlet of Brigflatts and the lovely old Quaker meeting house. Built in 1675, it is the second oldest in the country and, because of its association with the beginnings of Quakerism, is now one of the

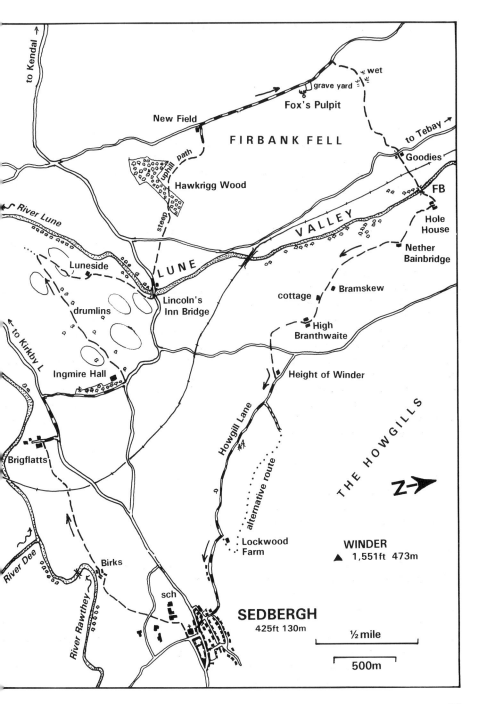

to Kendal →

grave yard
⚹ wet
Fox's Pulpit

New Field

FIRBANK FELL

to Tebay →

Goodies

path
uphill
steep

Hawkrigg Wood

FB

Hole House

VALLEY

Nether Bainbridge

River Lune

Luneside

L U N E

cottage
Bramskew

drumlins

Lincoln's Inn Bridge

High Branthwaite

to Kirkby L

Ingmire Hall

Height of Winder

Howgill Lane

THE HOWGILLS

Brigflatts

alternative route

N→

Lockwood Farm

WINDER
▲ 1,551ft 473m

River Dee

Birks

sch

SEDBERGH
425ft 130m

½ mile

500m

River Rawthey

93

most important buildings in the Sedbergh area, attracting a great deal of interest. The wooden gallery and unusual dog pen add character to the peaceful interior, where well-attended meetings for worship are held every Sunday morning. In the beautiful garden is the top of the old cross from Sedbergh market place, broken off by a mob when the Quaker William Dewsbury preached at it. Across the way, in the burial ground, lies the grave of Basil Bunting, the poet (1900-1985).

The farmhouse down the lane was where the Seeker, Richard Robinson lived, and where George Fox stayed after his vision on Pendle Hill. When asked where he came from, Fox said: 'from the Lord'. Richard Robinson must have wondered who he had in the house, and that night locked all the doors. In 1677, two years after the meeting house had been built, Fox revisited Brigflatts with his wife Margaret and daughter Rachel, when 500 people attended the meeting.

Turn right along the lane and left along the busy A683 for 350 yards (320m), then right onto Ingmire Back Lane – tree-lined further on. This is part of the Roman road which continued south to cross the River Rawthey at a deep ford called Lords Dub, only passable at low water. At the Kendal road, turn immediately left – signed 'Killington Bridge' – to pass Ingmire Hall and enter a parkland of large scattered trees and low rounded hills. The hills are drumlins, sculptured beneath an ice-sheet as it rode over the thick deposits of boulder clay.

Ingmire Hall was once the home of Sir John Otway who had a certain sympathy for the Quakers. In 1665 he arranged to have eleven Sedbergh Quakers released from York prison so that they could get the harvest in. The old Ingmire Hall was destroyed by fire in 1928.

Follow the footpath signs over a ladder stile and a drumlin with a finger post on top. At the next stile – between an oak and an alder – curve round to the right to a gate which leads into a hedge-lined lane. The rough ground has some interesting plants including climbing cordyalis, a delicate climbing plant with short spikes of creamy flowers. Beyond Luneside Farm, follow the field path to Lincolns Inn Bridge. The river here is rocky and wide, and makes a pleasant picnic spot.

Cross the narrow old stone bridge with its two graceful arches and, fifty yards (45m) past Lincolns Inn Farm, look out for a stile in the wall and turn steeply up to the right, following a field boundary. From the hill top there is a view of Waterside Viaduct, where the former railway crossed on a cast-iron arch with three arches of red sandstone on each side.

Go straight across the road – the B6257 – and up through a field which in spring is full of bulbous buttercups, to the edge of Hawk-rigg Wood where, to the left of some beeches, there is a stile into the wood. There are good views down the Lune Valley to the Lancaster Fells and across to the Howgills, Baugh Fell, Rise Hill, Whernside and Middleton Fell.

Pass diagonally up through the bluebell wood and then an ancient meadow, where more bluebells, yellow rattle, betony and devilsbit scabious grow, to reach the top left hand corner. You may also find baldpenny, that unusual but local member of the parsley family, rather like a cow parsley with feathery leaves.

Follow the yellow arrows through two wooden gates and turn right onto the road at New Field. It is about ⅔ mile (1km) along the ridge of Firbank Fell to Fox's Pulpit. On Firbank Fell you may see the redshank which breeds here. In flight it is recognisable by the broad white bar along the trailing edges of the wing and its white rump. When standing on a wall, the bright red legs, which give the bird its name, are easily seen. Its calls are particularly musical.

Fox's Pulpit is a rocky outcrop, marked by a commemorative plaque. It was here that George Fox came on that June day in 1652, the Sunday after he spoke at Sedbergh fair.

Of great historical importance, Brigflatts Quaker meeting house dates from 1675, and is still in use.

There was a small chapel here then which, on that morning, was full to overflowing to hear Francis Howgill and John Audland speak. But in the afternoon, about 1,000 people gathered and Fox spoke for three hours from the rock, now known as Fox's Pulpit. This historic event is regarded as the beginning of Quakerism. The chapel was damaged beyond repair in a storm in 1838, and the stone was used to build the new one lower down, overlooking the Lune and the How-gills.

Walk on to a cattle grid and turn right over a new stile, following the field boundary, through a boggy field to a sunken track and the road. The boggy area is permanent, but in July look for the yellow spikes of bog asphodel. It was here I was lucky to see a newly-emerged golden-ringed dragonfly which, when it was ready, rose into the air, its wings glittering like silver in the sun. The larval stage takes from four to five years before emerging as this beautiful insect.

Cross the road where there are some

Fox's Pulpit on Firbank Fell. The plaque reads: 'Let Your Lives Speak'.

cottages known as Goodies and, skirting the corner of a barn, go steeply down a field to the line of the old railway. Look for pieces of pink Shap granite among the ballast which was used for laying the track.

Drop down further to a magnificent new footbridge over the Lune, which carries Dales Way walkers across the river. Up the side beck to Hole House is a good site for wild flowers: butterbur, meadowsweet and wood stitchwort grow here, the latter with its feet in the running water; this pretty flower is distinguished from lesser stitchwort by its broader leaves.

Turn right through the neat, cobbled yard of Hole House and up across the farmyard to follow a sign over a low hill to 'Nether Bainbridge'. Turn right down the lane among beautiful scenery to Bramskew. Open country like this, with scattered trees, is ideal for the redstart. Its orange-red tail is unmistakable,

though you may first hear its call of *wee*, followed by a very quiet *ts ts*. They winter in West Africa, and a decline in population has been linked to droughts south of the Sahara.

Avoiding the 'Dales Way' gate, go through two metal gates and left of a barn, along the wall and lane to a footbridge and High Branthwaite Farm. Pass straight through the farmyard to follow a wall on the left up the hillside to Slacks Lane. Cross the road for the path to Height of Winder, turning right onto Howgill Lane. In summer this quiet, narrow road is bordered with ferns, quaking grass, herb bennet and honeysuckle.

It is about a mile (1.6km) along Howgill Lane into the market town of Sedbergh, but for an alternative scenic path on the edge of Winder, leave Howgill lane after 220 yards (200m) and turn up a double-walled track to the open fell, descending through Lockbank Farm.

WALK 15: THE CALF FROM CROOK O' LUNE BRIDGE

Start: Crook o' Lune Bridge. Grid Ref: 620 963
Distance: 9 miles (14km)
OS Maps: Pathfinder 617 or Landranger 97 and 98
Walking Time: 5 hours

A mountain climb to the highest point in the Howgills, combined with a river walk and a visit to the hamlet of Howgill. Crook o' Lune Bridge is near Lowgill, off the B6257, five miles (8km) north of Sedbergh onwards Tebay. There is space for one or two cars near the bridge or under the viaduct.

Crook o' Lune Bridge is a lovely old stone structure which spans the Lune in two graceful arches. It is very narrow, measuring just under seven feet (2.1m) between parapets, and is at least 300 years old; repairs were made in 1702, 1758 and 1817. Nearby is Davybank, an old corn mill built in 1746 with a now-disused water wheel. To the rear is the red sandstone 'eleven arches' railway viaduct of Lowgill, built on an elegant curve - also out of use. Until 1974, the river formed the boundary of Yorkshire and Westmorland, both now in Cumbria.

Lowgill Beck enters the Lune below the bridge and on the low-lying banks grow a profusion of flowers, the most spectacular being the giant bellflower. The tall flower spikes of pale milky blue appear in July and make a fine show on the riverbank.

Facing downstream on the bridge go left, along the road to a stile, to take the riverside footpath down the left bank of the river where open fields alternate with woods. You may meet walkers on their way from Ilkley to Bowness on Windermere as the path is part of the Dales Way.

Flowers grow in great variety and early woodland plants include bluebells, wild garlic and wood sorrel. By summer, they are replaced by enchanters nightshade, cow wheat and foxglove. By the river the showy imperforate St John's-wort has large yellow flowers on its square, winged stems and the petals have black dots on the surface. Melancholy thistle has no prickles and the backs of the broad leaves are white, the big flower-heads being a rich purple. Marsh woundwort is another large plant which has whorls of purple, two-lipped flowers on a loose spike, its leaves being long and narrow. Very similar is betony, which has narrow, heart-shaped leaves with rounded tips and crinkly margins. On the rocks, and almost in the water, grows creeping yellowcress.

You are likely to see dipper, heron and common sandpiper along the river. Dippers like to nest by a fast-flowing stream and are often first seen as they flit low over the water, alighting on a favourite rock or boulder. They bob and curtsy, then plunge into the surging water to seek out some tasty morsel. They even walk on the bed of the stream, hanging on with their sharp claws.

Cross the footbridge and take the lane to the left signed Howgill. A few houses, a former mill and the church make up the hamlet, cosily situated alongside Chapel Beck, round the green and off Howgill Lane. Howgill Mill was owned by the Best family and once employed over 100 people in the woollen trade. The simple church was built in 1838 replacing the original chapel (at Bantygill Cottage) founded in 1685 by John Robinson. On the hill is the former school, now the village hall.

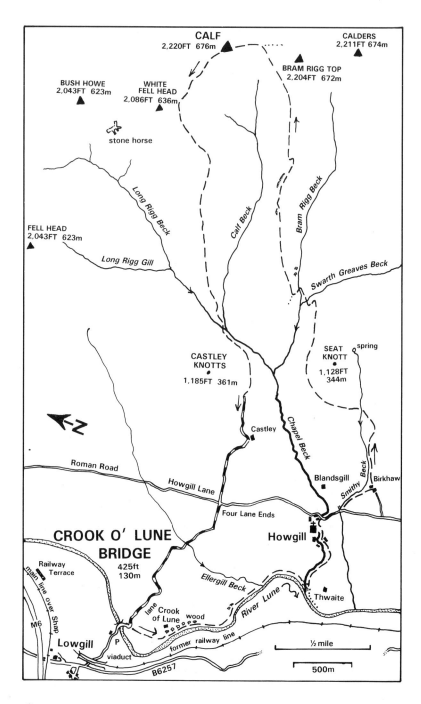

CALF
2,220FT 676m

CALDERS
2,211FT 674m

BRAM RIGG TOP
2,204FT 672m

BUSH HOWE
2,043FT 623m

WHITE
FELL HEAD
2,086FT 636m

stone horse

Long Rigg Beck

Calf Beck

Bram Rigg Beck

FELL HEAD
2,043FT 623m

Long Rigg Gill

Swarth Greaves Beck

N

CASTLEY
KNOTTS
1,185FT 361m

SEAT
KNOTT
1,128FT
344m

spring

Castley

Chapel Beck

Roman Road

Blandsgill

Smithy Beck

Birkhaw

Howgill Lane

Four Lane Ends

CROOK O' LUNE
BRIDGE
425ft
130m

Howgill

Railway
Terrace

Ellergill Beck

River Lune

Thwaite

main line over Shap

lane Crook
of Lune wood

M6

Lowgill

P

viaduct

former railway line

B6257

½ mile

500m

98

The lovely reddish-purple flowerheads of melancholy thistle grow on upright, tall stems, often on road verges or riverbanks.

Turn right onto Howgill Lane, up the hill to Blands Cottage, where a field path leads up the right side of Smithy Beck. This is part of the little parish of Bland, from which, it is said, every person in the world named Bland originates.

Seen from here, carved into the slopes of Bush Howe, is a now-neglected stone 'horse' which shows up as a dark patch on the hillside. Some people think it could have been made be the sea-going Norse, as it has been used by sailors to make landfall at Milnthorpe, fifteen miles (24km) away. Up to the early years of this century it was regularly cleaned on an annual visit by local farmers.

From Howgill Lane, go through the fields to Birkhaw Farm and a small wooden gate on the left of the farmhouse. Turn up the hill along the cart track and left, following the wall, towards the rocky knoll of Seat Knott.

Curving round to the right, descend to Bram Rigg Beck near a sheepfold. After 100 yards (90m) up from the beck, turn right to begin a steady climb up through the bracken-covered slopes to the ridge of Bram Rigg where there is another sheepfold. On the ridge, look skywards for that glossy black bird, the raven, which may be in the vicinity. There are also carrion crows too, of course, but the raven is larger, has a slower wing beat and a

The Calf; the 'stone horse' carved on the side of Bush Howe, to the left of the Calf, can just be seen.

deeper voice. At your feet you may see the slow-moving, shiny black dor beetle, on which these birds feed.

At the saddle, turn up to the left to scale the last gentle 130 feet (40m) to the summit of the Calf; the locals call it just 'Calf'. On a clear day there is a superb panoramic view. Wainwright describes it as unexcelled: 'There is not a more extensive panorama in England than this.' To the north is Cross Fell, the highest point on the Pennines. Nine Standards Rigg is visible, as are Wild Boar Fell and Baugh Fell. You can see the scarps of the beginning of Wensleydale, then further to the south are Penyghent, Ingleborough and Whernside with Morecambe Bay, and Killington Lake further round to the south-west. To the west are uninterrupted views of the Lake District mountains.

From the top of the Calf, take the path to White Fell, a north-westerly direction. Then curving left, follow the grassy track down the ridge. Half way down, from a few paces to the right, you can get a closer view of the stone horse on Bush Howe. It needs some imagination to see even which way it faces, as it seems to be reverting to a natural scar.

Descend to the beck, a lovely spot at the meeting place of two valleys where Calf Beck joins Chapel Beck. From here, the track curves round the hillside to a sheepfold and walled lane. Follow the lane past Castle Farm and Top Withens to Four Lane Ends. It was just before the cross-roads I first found baldpenny, that unusual, feathery-leaved member of the parsley family. Continue straight on down the road for another mile (1.6km) to Crook o' Lune Bridge.

WALK 16: CARLIN GILL AND BLACK FORCE

Start:	Carlingill Bridge. Grid Ref: 624 996
Distance:	7½ miles (12km)
OS Maps:	Pathfinder 617 or Landranger 97
Walking Time:	4 hours

For the sure-footed and energetic, this walk contains an exciting gill scramble and a wonderful high-level footpath on the west side of the Howgill Fells, with outstanding views down the Lune Valley to Morecambe Bay. The return is through farms and along the Roman road of Fair Mile. Carlin Gill is particularly rich in natural history. The starting point is best reached by turning off the Kendal to Tebay road near Low Borrowbridge – signed 'Carlin Gill'. There is space for parking off the road above the bridge.

Intriguing glimpses of the narrow, winding entrance to Carlin Gill – seen from the motorway – certainly invite a closer inspection, and this walk plumbs its depths. Its name means 'old woman ravine'. Early in its life – prior to the Ice Age – Carlin Gill probably flowed at a higher level, northwards, to join the Eden drainage. River capture took place early in the Ice Age (*see Rocks and the Landscape*) and the additional flow of water helped to carve out the Lune gorge.

Carlingill Bridge is the starting point of the walk. The single stone arch straddles a rocky gorge which, downstream, is hidden in the depths of a wooded ravine; upstream the gill is bare of trees. Start by walking up the side of the beck, soon crossing over to the left. Part of the fun of the gill is in making your own route, choosing whichever side of the beck seems best. Once the county boundary, the Yorkshire Dales National Park boundary follows the beck from the bridge to Blakethwaite Stone at the top of the gill.

Weasel Gill joins from the left, having built out a considerable stony delta for itself in times of flood. A little further on, a bare patch on the left bank reveals a mass of glacial till (or boulder clay), made up of boulders, cobbles, pebbles, sand and clay all mixed together. The only thing in nature that can produce such a mixture is moving ice, and only moving ice can cut scratches into the surface of boulders and pebbles, of which there are good examples here. The presence of these two phenomena are adequate proof that ice once covered this area. The Howgills had a comparatively small ice-cap and the movement of the ice was slow, so debris was not carried very far and Carlin Gill became choked with glacial till.

The rocky areas are frequently colonised by bunches of parsley fern and New Zealand willowherb. The fern has two kinds of leaf or frond, a longer fertile one and a more parsley-like sterile frond, while the tiny willowherb, once grown as a rockery plant, is now finding a place for itself where little else will grow. As you go up the beck you may disturb a heron, which finds the fishing good, and in the beck itself you may notice some dirty-white blobs attached to the rocks. These are fresh-water sponges and known as river sponge. They are members of the animal kingdom, and collect oxygen and food particles from the water as it flows over them

As the valley floor narrows, Green Knott Gill enters from the left and Small Gill from the right. Beyond this, the beck has a solid rock bed again. Clinging to damp ledges you may find yellow mountain saxifrage, a flower of the upland which likes a cool climate and is not found below 1,000 feet (300m). Its

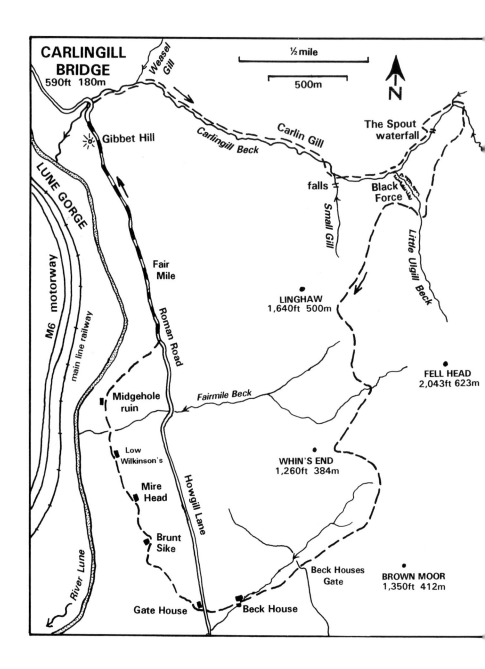

CARLINGILL
BRIDGE
590ft 180m

½ mile

500m

N

Weasel Gill

Gibbet Hill

Carlingill Beck

Carlin Gill

The Spout
waterfall

falls

Black
Force

LUNE GORGE

M6 motorway

main line railway

Fair
Mile

Roman Road

Small Gill

Little Ulgill Beck

LINGHAW
1,640ft 500m

FELL HEAD
2,043ft 623m

Midgehole
ruin

Fairmile Beck

Low
Wilkinson's

Mire
Head

WHIN'S END
1,260ft 384m

Howgill Lane

Brunt
Sike

River Lune

Beck Houses
Gate

BROWN MOOR
1,350ft 412m

Gate House

Beck House

The yellow mountain saxifrage is true to its name – it only grows above 1,000 feet (300m).

:aves are fleshy and the petals orange-
:llow. Growing with it are hard fern and
1aidenhair spleenwort and, in the shelter of
1e gorge, a few small ash, elm and rowan
·ees.

In the gorge the rock layers dip steeply as
1e sides close in, and an exciting scramble
·nsues. The steep and narrow ravine of Black
·orce enters from the right where Little Ulgil
3eck plunges down an impressive staircase of
ocks and falls, the summer home of ring
1zel. Continue up to the Spout, a well-
amed shoot of a waterfall thirty feet (10m)
igh and almost hidden behind a steep ledge
f rock where it blocks the main gorge. In
arly summer the cliffs are decked with
:abious, St John's-wort, valerian and golden
od.

From the foot of the waterfall, scramble up
the left side – there are steep footholds in the
turf – and a brief zigzag brings you to a point
above the falls. The next feature is where the
valley divides. Go up the right hand fork –
Great Uldale Beck – to where a worn track
comes in from the left. Cross the beck to the
right, and climb up the steep grassy bank
opposite (avoid the lower sheep track) to find
a good path high above Carlin Gill and
heading to the upper end of Black Force,
where the rock strata exhibit a fine downfold
or syncline.

Pause occasionally to cast your eyes sky-
ward. You may have already seen a buzzard
soaring up there and you can look out too,
and listen, for ravens and peregrines. The
raven's deep-throated *purrk* is easy to

Oystercatchers make nesting sites in pebble 'scrapes' alongside rivers and streams.

remember but the peregrine also has a call, a harsh *kee-errk*, not unlike the sound of a gull. On the ground you may see a large, fat, shiny beetle slowly crossing your path. This is the dor beetle, one of the dung beetles that tidy up the countryside. When flying, the beetle makes a droning sound from which it gets its name – *dor* being an old word meaning drone.

Cross Little Ulgill Beck, which flows into the chasm of Black Force, and go up the steep track opposite and round the hillside of Blake

The view down Carlin Gill, a stream-eroded V-shaped valley, looking towards the Lune gorge.

Ridge – still with precipitous views into Carlin Gill – to the col and different, extensive views to the south. The lower Lune Valley and Morecambe Bay spread into the distance, and the nuclear power station at Heysham is in view.

From the col (or saddle), go straight on along a fine track which makes excellent walking – short green turf and a slight downhill gradient – round the head of Blind Gill, and gently double back over the next ridge of Whins End to descend to Ellergill Beck. Cross the stream, but avoid the path which climbs straight on; turn right, high on the left side of Ellergill Beck, to descend further to a wall corner known as Beck Houses Gate.

On approaching Beck House, cross the beck to pass through the farmyard and on to the concrete drive to Howgill Lane. The next mile (1.6km) of footpath passes through four or five farms and regains the road again further north.

The farmland here is home to the yellow-hammer, one of our most colourful year-round residents. Not only the swifts and swallows make use of the old farm buildings, but the little owl may find a hole to nest. The little owl feeds on insects, small mammals and the occasional bird. This day-flying owl is often seen perched on a post.

Cross Howgill Lane, straight through Gate House farmyard and, turning in the up-valley direction, continue to Brunt Sike – meaning burnt ground by a stream – passing to the right of it. Still without losing height, go though fields and over a ladder stile to pass below the farmhouse of Mire Head. At Low Wilkinson's, go through the farmyard and straight on, crossing a footbridge hidden among the trees. Fairmile Beck seems to follow a deep cleft in the rock here. Pass the abandoned farm of Midgehole (now used as a barn) – the name means a soft boggy place – and round to a gate. There are fine views of the river below and the Lune gorge beyond. Strike up through the bracken to the road.

Turn left for one mile (1.6km) along Fairmile Road to complete the walk. This is the route of the old Roman road from Ribchester (in Lancashire) to Carlisle. A section of the road here was found to be eighteen feet (5.5m) wide with a foundation of large stones on yellow clay, with a four inch (10cm) thick, closely-packed surface layer. Only three miles to the north was the fort of Low Borrowbridge, which guarded the Lune gorge (*see walk 17*). Fairmile takes its name from the sheep and horse fairs that were held here. Just before reaching Carlingill Bridge, pass Gibbet Hill, a prominent mound topped by a cairn. Human bones have been found here, and on dark nights the clanking of chains was once heard as the unfortunate body of a sheep stealer swung in the wind. Nearby, among the bracken and harebells, mushrooms grow in unusually large fairy rings.

WALK 17: BORROWDALE AND BREAST HIGH FROM TEBAY

Start: Tebay. Grid Ref: 616 044
Distance: 12½ miles (20km)
OS Maps: Pathfinder 607 and Outdoor Leisure 7 or Landranger 90
Walking Time: 6½ hours

In this little-known area on the fringe of the Lake District, the busy motorway contrasts with the peaceful isolation of two of the River Lune's tributary dales. The route visits a site for orchids, passes through the Lune gorge and the Roman fort of Low Borrowbridge. It explores the lonely, winding valley of Borrowdale, before turning up over Breast High into Bretherdale and returning via Greenholme. Tebay is off junction 38 on the M6. There is parking space to the rear of the church.

Tebay is well-known as the railway village. The North Eastern line, running to Kirkby Stephen and Darlington, was closed in 1962 and Tebay Station, on the main line to Scotland, closed six years later. Tebay had lost the reason for its existence. The church was built in 1880 for a growing population of railway workers, the font being chiselled from a solid block of Shap granite.

The group of cottages of Old Tebay – the name means 'Tibba's water meadow' – lies in a hollow by the River Lune, below the large roundabout which leads onto the motorway. An ugly old lady named Mary Baines, who once lived here, was blamed for just about every accident or strange thing that occurred in the district, from the milk turning sour to a horse bolting. However, she did predict that, some day, carriages would run over Shap without the help of horses. Mary Baines died in 1811 aged ninety.

Starting from the church, walk further down the road, Church Street, and a lane to the footbridge over the river. (From the car park behind the church, go down through the stiles over the former railway to join the lane.) The River Lune has just swung round to the south and is about to start its journey through the Lune gorge.

From the footbridge go down-river, pass under the railway and motorway along a byroad to Roundthwaite, a group of farms and cottages on the banks of Roundthwaite Beck. Follow the minor road to the junction with the A685. In early summer, the roadside embankments here are covered in orchids, the common spotted orchid – mostly pale pinks or even white – and northern marsh orchid – deep reds. It is likely that many of the tall, strong plants are hybrids of the two. Among the orchids are patches of bugle, oxeye daisy and birdsfoot trefoil.

Cross the motorway and railway along the new bridge to a farm track leading off to the right. Just upstream is the old Lunes Bridge, which spans a narrow rocky gorge where the river rushes over the steeply dipping Silurian strata. The single stone arch is no longer in use as a bridge though, when the salmon are running, it serves as a car park for fishermen.

The next mile (1.6km) of the walk is through the narrowest part of the gorge, where the valley sides rise up steeply. The gorge was probably started by the river before the Ice Age, then deepened by ice to its present shape, with a further notch carved into the rocky floor by the river.

From the farm track which leads to Brockholes Farm, there is a view of the modern bridge you have just crossed and which replaced the old Lunes Bridge. It carries the road not just over the river, but over the

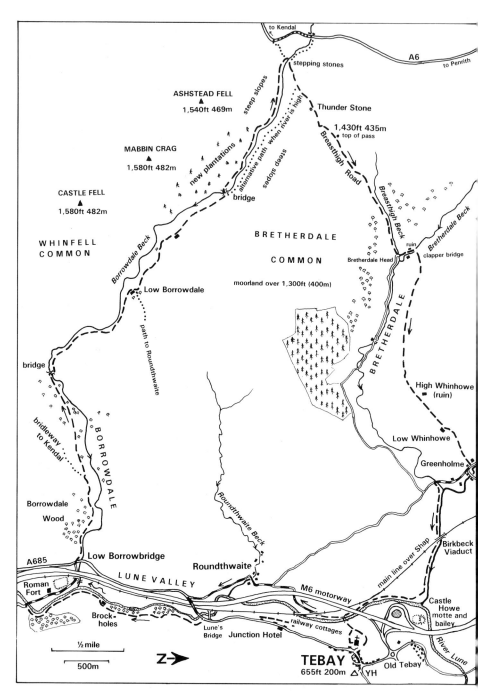

ASHSTEAD FELL
1,540ft 469m

MABBIN CRAG
1,580ft 482m

CASTLE FELL
1,580ft 482m

WHINFELL
COMMON

to Kendal

stepping stones

A6
to Penrith

Thunder Stone

1,430ft 435m
top of pass

steep slopes

new plantations

alternative path when river is high

scabous seats

bridge

Breasthigh Road

Breasthigh Beck

Bretherdale Beck

ruin

clapper bridge

Bretherdale Head

BRETHERDALE
COMMON

moorland over 1,300ft (400m)

BRETHERDALE

Borrowdale Beck

Low Borrowdale

path to Roundthwaite

High Whinhowe
(ruin)

Low Whinhowe

bridge

bridleway
to Kendal

BORROWDALE

Greenholme

Borrowdale
Wood

Roundthwaite Beck

main line over Shap

Birkbeck
Viaduct

A685

Low Borrowbridge

Roundthwaite

LUNE VALLEY

M6 motorway

Castle
Howe
motte and
bailey

Roman
Fort

Brock-
holes

½ mile

500m

Z→

railway cottages

Lune's
Bridge

Junction Hotel

River Lune

TEBAY
655ft 200m △ YH

Old Tebay

railway and motorway, too, in a beautiful sweeping curve, mounted on slender pillars. On completion of the motorway from Lancaster to Penrith in 1971, the Civic Trust gave it an award for 'an outstanding contribution to the appearance of the Westmorland landscape'.

From the path, nearer to Brockholes, a view across to the motorway shows how the engineering of the far carriageway has revealed a section in the Silurian strata with the sharp folds of a syncline and an anticline. A further technological achievement is met with near the farm where there are signs of a newly-laid pipeline which carries ethylene from Edinburgh to Merseyside. The Lune gorge is thus a vital line of communication, as it has been for more than 2,000 years.

Go through the farmyard of Brockholes, along the top of the riverbank and into a short stretch of attractive deciduous woodland where, in spring, there is a display of bluebells, yellow pimpernel and herb bennet. By autumn, the trees are a riot of yellows, browns and reds. At the road, turn over Salterwath Bridge, two low-slung stone arches, from where you may see grey wagtail, dipper or common sandpiper active along the rushing river below. The name Salterwath – meaning salter's ford – is a reminder that it was once on the salt packhorse route from Kendal north.

Pass Borrowbridge Farm (formerly an inn) where, on the left and just beyond the farm, is the playing-card shaped raised platform of a Roman fort with embankments on two sides. It measures 140 feet (42m) long and 120 feet (36m) wide and would have held 500 soldiers. Situated in this strategic position, the fort was built to guard the Lune gap on the road north to Carlisle. It is not known what name the Romans gave this camp, but it was probably built in the second century AD, perhaps replacing a smaller one. There have been few finds, until Shell built the ethylene pipeline when, just north of the fort, a Roman

cemetery was uncovered. It contained sixty cremation burial urns and one tombstone of a cavalryman called Aurelius who lived to be thirty-five. Low Borrow Bridge itself crosses Borrow Beck on the right, on the line of the old road just before the beck joins the Lune.

Pass under the stone arches of the railway viaduct, under the motorway and cross the A685. From here begins a fine bridleway up Borrowdale. This little-known, Westmorland Borrowdale – the famous one being south of Keswick in the Lake District – is a very quiet valley among lonely hills, where you will see few people. Some years ago, the dale survived a plan to flood it to make a reservoir, but the only recent change is the addition of some afforestation on the Whinfell Common side of the dale, where the young trees are becoming well-established.

The track starts up Borrow Beck and through Borrowdale Wood, an ancient woodland of oak, ash and alder which, further on, thins out to scattered trees. At a stone bridge, a bridleway leads over the hills towards Kendal.

The track crosses Borrow Beck where the valley turns direction and where the beck cuts deeply into glacial and river debris. Eelman Sike, a broad hollow ahead, contains several glacial mounds though, further on, where Borrow Beck cuts into its bank, it reveals sorted layers of pebbles and sand, indicating deposition by the river not by ice. Two levels of river terraces can be made out along the valley.

Go through the farmyard of Low Borrowdale, the only working farm in the dale. (If required, a shortened return route may be taken from here by turning right behind the farmhouse and climbing steeply over Belt Howe to Roundthwaite.)

Continue up the valley to High Borrowdale, long since abandoned and now a sad ruin; and on to a bridge over the beck. Among the birdlife to look out for are the secretive common sandpiper, the grey wagtail and, among the rocks and ruins, the handsome wheatear, while overhead the buzzard and raven may be conspicuous. By providing a good habitat for small mammals, the young forestry plantation makes a good hunting ground for birds of prey.

The main track crosses the bridge to follow the left bank of the beck, almost as far as the main A6 road, where it meets another path from the left which crosses the beck at some stepping stones. (If the river is full and difficult to cross, walk up to the main road and down the far bank.)

Turning direction, follow the ancient track of Breasthigh Road diagonally up the hillside to the Thunder Stone. This large glacial erratic of Shap granite, lying just beyond the metal gate, has travelled a mere three miles (5km) from the granite outcrop to the north. However, its seven or eight tons must some-how have become entombed in the ice, later

The Thunder Stone is a large granite boulder alongside an ancient packhorse route. The Whinfell Hills and Borrowdale form its backdrop.

to be left perched here in this scenic spot high above Borrowdale. There are one or two other 'thunder stones' in the area, such as the one at the head of Bretherdale. They were thought to have been placed there by thun derbolts.

From the summit of the pass over Breast High, on a clear day there is a magnificent view of the Pennines, the limestone of Orton Scar and, immediately below, the lovely vale of Bretherdale, in spring its hillsides dotted with May blossom.

Descend to join the beck and, at the road turn left, skirting Bretherdale Head Farm and passing through the ruins of another aban doned farmhouse to a unique footbridge made of three huge slabs of Silurian slate Curve round to the right, through two or three gates, for some good walking on a little used old track cut into the valley side, with views down Bretherdale. The far side of the dale is clothed with deciduous then conifer ous woods.

Cross a minor road and continue, taking the left of two gates, straight on past the ruins of High Whinnhowe and down to Low Whinnhowe, again along an old track. Carry on to the peaceful little hamlet of Green holme, a few cottages, chapel and village hall clustered next to Birk Beck which widens along the edge of the green to become the village 'pond'.

Turn right along the road, following the Tebay sign and, immediately after a bridge over Bretherdale Beck, turn left along its bank, signed 'Tebay'. The stream soon joins Birk Beck, coming in from the left, and the pleasant path leads along the beckside under one of the the stone arches of Birkbeck Viaduct. On the railway embankment grow a fine show of flowers including melancholy thistle, pink purslane, oxeye daisy, wood cranesbill and meadowsweet.

Turning south, where Birk Beck joins the Lune, there is a good view of Castle Howe a Norman motte and bailey just over the river

The buzzard is the largest bird of the open moors, and can be seen most often in spring and summer, soaring and circling in unhurried, effortless flight as it hunts for small mammals.

now a green hump and platform. This would have been a wooden fort with a courtyard in front of it, built soon after 1066. It is possible to approach it on foot from Old Tebay.

Continue along the bank of the Lune, close to the river and under the motorway to the footbridge. Cross the river here to return up the road and back into Tebay.

WALK 18: SHAP WELLS FROM GREENHOLME

Start: Greenholme. Grid Ref: 597 057
Distance: 8½ miles (13½km)
OS Maps: Outdoor Leisure 7 or Landranger 90
Walking Time: 4½ hours

This can be a wild walk, and is best undertaken on a clear day with a brisk wind from the west to blow away the noise of the motorway. It follows Birk Beck, the northernmost tributary of the Lune, passes by Shap Wells Hotel, climbs gently up onto Birkbeck Fell to Stakely Pike at 1,300 feet (400m) above sea level, and descends along the ridge back to Greenholme. Map and compass are advisable. The main interest is the geology of the Shap area. The quiet little hamlet of Greenholme is just half a mile (800m) from Tebay West service station on the northbound M6. There is space for a few cars, but the walk could equally well be started from the motorway service station. To reach Greenholme, go past the motel and turn left at the t-junction.

Greenholme is an untouched, almost forgotten hamlet where Birk Beck attractively opens out to form a 'duck pond' at its centre. The village hall, Methodist church, farms and cottages are grouped unceremoniously round a wide green. It lies on the old Roman road north, a route in use through medieval times to the eighteenth century when packhorse trains called here, and wayside inns welcomed travellers.

To start the walk, cross the bridge over the beck, walk up the road for 330 yards (300m) and turn left, through a metal gate, across the fields, up the side of the beck to Steps Farm. Cross back over the beck and continue along the byroad. In summer, the streamside is decorated with the purple flowers of fairy foxglove, a plant that sometimes provides a splash of colour to old ruins and walls, as on the old castle walls at Middleham in Wensleydale.

Just beyond Scout Green, take the farm track on the left. Scattered about are several boulders of Shap granite, known as erratics. They don't match the underlying rock and can only have been transported here by being carried within, or on, glacier ice. Shap granite is so distinctive and easily identified that it is very useful in reconstructing the story of the

Ice Age, especially the direction the ice moved and how far it travelled. The large feldspar crystals often resist weathering and jut out of the surface of the boulder like currants in a bun.

After 110 yards (100m) along the farm track, turn right onto some higher ground over Green Brow to a stile in the far left corner of the field, then keep near to the beck – and to the right of a fence – for the next half mile (800m). You will hear the waterfall of Docker Force hidden in a deep wooded ravine; the path is along the top. The woods are of alder, rowan and especially birch, hence the name Birk Beck. Curlews like the rough farmland, where they find nest sites on the ground among the tussocks of grass. This streaky brown bird with a long curved bill may be seen in its song flight, gliding along and calling out its bubbling, liquid notes, one of the most evocative and memorable of bird calls.

At the end of the woodland, cross the stile in the wall into a meadow, and climb up to the crest of the ridge to the left of the farmhouse. Go through the farmyard and up the farm track to the railway – the main line from London to Glasgow. The highest point on the line – Shap summit – is just 1½ miles

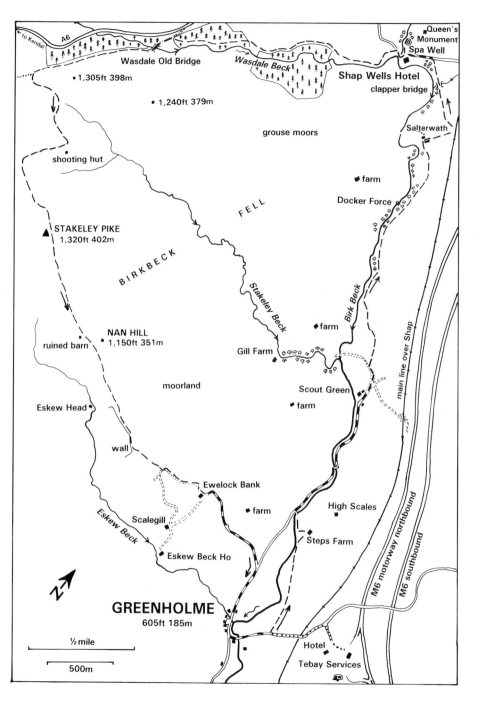

to Kendal A6

1,305ft 398m

Wasdale Old Bridge

Wasdale Beck

Queen's Monument
Spa Well

Shap Wells Hotel
clapper bridge

1,240ft 379m

grouse moors

Salterwath

shooting hut

farm

Docker Force

FELL

STAKELEY PIKE
1,320ft 402m

BIRKBECK

Stakeley Beck

Birk Beck

NAN HILL
1,150ft 351m

ruined barn

farm

Gill Farm

main line over Shap

moorland

Eskew Head

Scout Green

farm

wall

High Scales

Ewelock Bank

Scalegill

farm

Eskew Beck

Eskew Beck Ho

Steps Farm

M6 motorway northbound

M6 southbound

N

GREENHOLME
605ft 185m

½ mile

500m

Hotel

Tebay Services

(2.5km) further north where the railway is 916 feet (280m) above sea level. Trains going north are part way along a steep, four mile (6.4km) incline (of 1 in 75) from Tebay to Shap summit.

Turn left, away from the railway and towards Shap Wells Hotel – nestled in a hollow – crossing a field of rushes and scattered granite boulders to a wooden gate. Cross Trundle Beck by an ancient stone slab bridge, beneath which the reddish rock is near the base of the Carboniferous succession.

Go up the track to Shap Wells Hotel. On the hill is Queens Monument, erected in 1842 to commemorate Queen Victoria's accession (of 1837). The twenty-three foot (7m) column is topped by a six foot (1.85m) statue of the queen. A path from the hotel car park leads to Spa Well, past the old bath house. In Victorian times, people came to bathe in or drink the waters. The old well is no longer in use but the spring water issues from the riverbank.

The hotel opened in 1833 and was rebuilt in 1915. During the second World War it became a prisoner-of-war camp for German officers, many of whom returned later to stay at the hotel. Two of the officers made a daring, almost successful, escape in a laundry basket. They made their way to an aerodrome near Carlisle, stole a small plane but, having run out of fuel, were forced down in mist near Great Yarmouth.

From the front of the hotel, cross the bridge and walk up the right side of the beck which, having changed direction, has changed its name to Wasdale Beck.

It is quite likely you may have the company of a party of geology students, as this is an important locality. Across the beck is an outcrop of pinkish-brown rock which dips gently downstream. This is the initial bed (the basal conglomerate) of the Carboniferous system of strata (350 million years old) and here it contains pink feldspar crystals, eroded at the time from the nearby granite. It follows that this material could only have accumulated after the granite had cooled and been uncovered by erosion, therefore the granite is older than the conglomerate.

A few yards higher up, near the waterfall, the conglomerate is seen to rest on almost vertical, black, Silurian siltstones (420 million years old). This 'unconformity' – where the two rock types lie at different angles, one on top of the other – represents a gap of seventy million years of geological time, where a whole volume of earth history is missing – all of the Devonian strata.

A few yards above the waterfall, holes have been drilled into the Silurian siltstone. This is where core samples have been taken to measure 'fossil' magnetism in the rock, research which led to the discovery of our wandering continents. The direction and dip of the magnetic north, fossilised in the rock, indicates that the British area was somewhere south of the Equator in Silurian times.

In spring, the marshy areas have a good show of wet-loving plants. Among them are birdseye primrose, two louseworts, ragged robin, butterwort and heath spotted orchid. A member of the foxglove family, marsh lousewort is also known as red rattle which refers, both to the pinkish-purple flowers, and to the deep red colour of much of the plant itself. The common lousewort is smaller and the flowers are a paler purple. They both grow in damp, acid conditions. The name comes from the belief that sheep became infected by lice from the plant. Higher up the fellside, on the left, are heather-covered moors where the fragrant bog myrtle and delicate cranberry grow.

Continue upstream to a spruce plantation and turn up along the right side of it. At the end of the plantation, ignore the inviting footbridge and climb gradually up to a stile and enter a second plantation, passing straight through it on a rough path to emerge onto a track that leads down left to Wasdale

The peregrine likes high, rocky cliffs for nesting. Open moorland is the ideal ground for this falcon to hunt, and once it has spotted its prey, it will stoop in a headlong dive with wings closed together, reaching speeds of 95 to 155 mph (150-250kph).

Bright yellow kingcups grow in damp fields and wet places.

Old Bridge. This route is an old one which was used by Scottish drovers and packponies, and names like Packhorse Hill, Dryside, Wolf Howe and Muddy Brow conjure up conditions along the way.

If you have been keeping an eye open for birdlife, you may have already seen buzzard, peregrine, kestrel or sparrowhawk. It is wild country and the scattered plantations often have populations of field voles which attract the birds of prey.

Go up the track, to the left of the next plantation, and, as you come onto the open fell, look across to the pink rock quarry, the only one where Shap granite is obtained. The beautiful polished stone is used all over the country for the facing of banks and other important buildings, and for gravestones.

About 150 yards (140m) beyond the conifers, turn left through a gate, on a track across the fells. On a clear day there are fine distant views across to the Pennines and the

Eden Valley, Wild Boar Fell and the Howgills. Follow the track round, leaving the rusty shooting hut over to the left, and continue across a line of grouse butts, to the viewpoint and little cairn on Stakeley Pike, 1,300 feet (400m) above sea level. The track continues to the left of this rocky eminence, but if mist comes down take a bearing of 110° (from north) from Stakeley Pike.

The track aims for a ruined barn with Tebay village in the distance, passing between Nan Hill and the ruin. From here, the crest of the ridge is to the left and to the right is a view into a small valley with scattered barns and trees, drained by Eskew Beck. Keeping above the intake wall, bear left at the wall corner and left again at a t-junction of tracks, to take you down to Ewelock Bank Farm. From here, the easiest return to Greenholme is left along the unfenced, tarred road.

WALK 19: ORTON AND GREAT ASBY SCAR

Start:	Orton. Grid Ref: 622 082
Distance:	11 miles (17½km)
OS Maps:	Pathfinder 607 and 597 or Landranger 91
Walking Time:	5½ hours

This walk explores the delightful villages of Orton and Great Asby and the remarkable limestone upland of Orton Scar where there are fine limestone pavements. Walking is easy-going, paths generally good and views extensive. The Lune is left behind for a glimpse of the Eden. There is parking in the centre of Orton, which lies two miles (3km) north of Tebay on the Kendal to Appleby road (B6260). The walk may be shortened by two miles (3km), cutting out Great Asby.

Situated high in the Lune Valley at over 750 feet (230m) above sea level, Orton is a charming village of great historical interest. The former green is now the car park, but the village is well spread out and has a much larger 'green' consisting of meadows and the school playing field, where two lovely clear streams wind their way. The most ancient inhabited building is Hall Farm, an impressive stone house dated 1604; on the south side of the village is Orton Hall, renamed Petty Hall in the seventeenth century by Christopher Petty of Storiths (near Bolton Abbey in Wharfedale). The church was largely restored in 1877, though the fine tower dates from 1504.

Orton is the focus of seven roads and several public footpaths, all of which converge on this little community, evidence of a more important past. In fact, Orton was once a market town with its own charter, and a great annual event was the Whitsun fair, originally granted at the request of Lady Anne Clifford. Handloom weaving and knitting became important occupations, and Kendal market was the destination of hundreds of pairs of knitted stockings every week, bringing a useful income to the hard-working inhabitants. Today there is a village store and a tea room, and you may be tempted to visit the small chocolate factory.

Orton is noted for an unsolved murder. A gravestone in the churchyard tells the tale of Thomas Hunter, who was waylaid, shot and robbed. It was November 1837 and he was making his way home from Kendal on his carrier's cart, 'Thomas Hunter of Archer Hill was cut down as a flower in the 32nd year of his age'.

There is also a legend of the Orton dobbie, a kind of poltergeist. It all started about 1850 in an old farmhouse. People came from far and wide to try to catch a glimpse of this strange phenomenon; priests tried to exorcise it and some locals actively encouraged the ghost story to attract money from visitors.

The first part of the walk has several twists and turns, so needs care in following and may require some map reading. To start, go along the Appleby road and turn first right, then left to Mill House Farm. Turn right through the farmyard, then left along a green lane with low walls. At a crossways of green lanes, turn right and go through the left of two metal gates to the top corner of an ancient meadow, then though a rusty gate into a lovely damp patch. Here in spring, a surprising collection of flowers form a rich botanical corner, part of Orton Meadows – a Site of Special Scientific Interest. Among the less common are birdseye primrose, common spotted orchid and the beautiful large yellow blooms

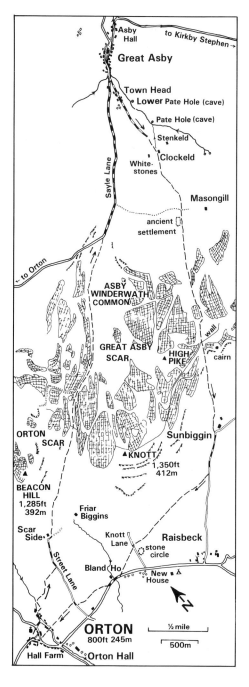

of globeflower. By late summer these are replaced by devilsbit scabious, saw-wort betony and that delectable, cream-coloured flower, grass of Parnassus. Saw-wort is rather like a delicate knapweed in appearance, a plant once useful in providing a yellow-green dye for wool.

Continue up through a small gate and along to Street Lane. Turn left along the lane where, in summer, field scabious can be distinguished from devilsbit scabious by its flatter flower heads and unequal sized florets.

Immediately past Scar Farm, turn up (first a gate then a step stile) diagonally through field gates to continue above a wall to a packhorse-sized gap in a wall. On the south-facing limestone bank grows a very special flower – the carline thistle. A plant of lowland Britain, this must be one of the most north-erly places where this plant can grow as it only produces fertile seed in the warmest sum-mers. It is a small, squat thistle with multiple yellow-brown flower heads. The dead flowers dry out and can survive into the winter.

Continue roughly in the same uphill direction to a stile by a metal water trough and eventually up to a gate and rough grazing land. The view back of the Lune Valley and the northern Howgills is magnificent and panoramic. It compares well with other fine views of the Howgills like those from from Longstone Common or Firbank Fell. Over to the left you can just see the cross of the Jubilee Monument to Queen Victoria on Beacon Hill.

Keeping the same direction, the limestone scars close in on the footpath from the right and left until a stile in a wall is reached near the left scar. This is roughly the highest point on this leg of the walk, and marks a division between land behind that drains south to the Lune and the slopes ahead where streams drain to the Eden and the north.

The route ahead follows a low grassy belt between wide stretches of amazing scenery where limestone pavements form broad tables of rock, tilted this way and that. The rock was laid bare by the action of ice riding over it during the Ice Age and, in the last 10,000 years since the ice melted, little soil has accumulated because the limestone is pure and soluble, leaving little debris to form soil. Here is a chance to explore the botany of the clefts or grikes in the pavements. The ferns and flowers to be found make a fascinating study and include harts tongue, black and green spleenwort, limestone polypody and wall rue; woodland plants such as dog's mercury, wood sorrel and herb robert grow well in the sheltered environment. The tiny blue-leaved saxifrage grows in the ledges near the light while in the open, cushions of wild thyme add colour to a natural rockery.

Descend through limestone then bracken to a wall which comes in from the right. Walk alongside it to a fine step stile, then a gate, as you cross Asby Winderworth Common. In the late summer you will come across several kinds of mushroom and toadstool. The edible field mushroom is delicious and grows to a large size. Check that the gills are pink in the young button mushroom, brown and dark brown in older ones. There are the larger horse mushrooms which also make good eating, and puff balls are fairly common.

The route then leads into a green lane where, beyond a gate on the left, a well-built entrance to a leadmine can be seen. Join Sayle Lane, a quiet road with wonderful verges full of wild flowers. (For the shorter version of the walk, after 500 yards (450m) along the road turn right, over a cattle grid, on a meadowside farm track. Turn right again at the fingerpost to rejoin the main route.)

Another mile (1.6km) along the lane brings you into Great Asby. This 'village by the ash trees' stands on either side of Asby Gill. The walled St Helens Well in the centre of the village and St Thomas's Well lower down add copious springs of clear water to the often dry beck. The church of 1866 stands on an island, round which the beck divides. Some

Harts tongue fern is easily identified by its broad, fleshy leaves.

of the houses and cottages are very old, Asby Hall, dated 1694, being the most impressive.

In his book *A Portrait of the Howgills and the Upper Eden Valley*, Michael Ffinch recalls that the rectory has an ancient pele tower built into it where the parson could escape passing marauders. The building also has a Lady Anne Clifford lock, dated 1670. On their way from Appleby to Pendragon Castle, Lady Anne and her household were forced to take shelter here during a violent storm and the lock, made by George Dent of Appleby, was presented for kindness shown.

Surprisingly, there is only a mobile shop for this large village, though the Three Greyhounds pub provides welcome food and drink.

For the return route to Orton, walk back up the village and fork left up Town Head Lane. To the left Asby Gill runs in a small ravine where there are two caves. Pate Hole is 1,500 feet (457m) long with a wide entrance, and nearer to the village is Lower

Limestone pavements on Great Asby Scar, before the route descends to Sunbiggin Farm.

Pate Hole with an entrance that soon narrows and a depth of only 80 feet (24m). After rain, Pate Hole becomes completely flooded, providing more water for the beck.

Pass through Clockeld Farm. The Norse word *keld* means spring and this is another water source. Keep first to the wall, then cross to a stile over to the left. From here to Sunbiggin, the East Cumbria Countryside Project have waymarked the route and provided it with excellent stiles and gates.

After crossing the track from Sayle Lane and about 100 yards (90m) along, the uneven ground on the right is evidence of an ancient settlement. Cowslip and pignut grow here in the spring and, later on, small scabious, the third member of this attractive family of bluish-purple flowers. Scabious was so named because it was thought to be a cure for the scabs and other skin complaints.

Follow the wall, then fence, to the lime stone and the summit ridge. From the highest part of the scar there is a wonderful panorama of Wild Boar Fell and the Howgills, giving feeling of wide open spaces. This is part of national nature reserve on the limeston pavements. To the left is Little Asby Scar which gave the name 'Asbian' to a sub division of the Carboniferous period and is used by geologists the world over. This is very quiet area and, for company, you may only have the curlew, raven or carrion crow though you are quite likely to see a buzzard patrolling the scars in its search for foo

...ton Church has a fine tower dating from 1504.

crystals sometimes jut out like currants in a bun. The thirty stones describe a circle some 120 feet (36m) across, which lies in a most delightful position in a meadow at the foot of the limestone scars. Like other stone circles it is probably of the Bronze Age (2,000-600 BC). The farmer in whose field it lies finds it a problem to mow the grass and would prefer not to have it.

You may have seen other Shap granite boulders along this walk. It is surprising how, during the Ice Age, glaciers distributed lumps of the granite so far afield. They have been found in the moraines south of York and as far away as the Yorkshire coast, yet this distinctive rock comes from just one small circular outcrop on Shap Fell less than one square mile ($2\frac{1}{2}km^2$) in area.

Cross Knott Lane and go over a stile, a few paces to the left, and a path diagonally across a large meadow to the road. If the meadow is in hay, it is preferable to go down the lane and along the road. Typical of the upper Lune valley, there are wide grass verges, a haven for a large variety of wild flowers; in the early summer, pinkish-purple clumps of wood cranesbill are prominent.

Soon after Bland House, leave the road by the stile on the right and go diagonally to a wall corner, then straight through a series of stiles to Street Lane. Turn right along the lane, then left over a stile to follow a wall directly to Orton. At the wall's end, find a narrow path called Cuckoo Lane, to bring you into the village. Carry on across the road where a footbridge crosses a crystal-clear stream which, in summer, is lined with monkeyflower. Go by the playing field to reach the centre of Orton village.

...dents and small rabbits. The soaring flight characteristic, and it is often chased by ...her birds.

The descent brings you to the hamlet of ...unbiggin, a group of farms, then, after a ...ird of a mile (550m) along the road, turn ...ght opposite Acres, through double gates on ...bridleway to Knott Lane and the stone ...rcle. With the exception of a block of ...mestone, the stones are large, rounded Shap ...anite boulders – the large pink feldspar

WALK 20: GREEN BELL AND THE SOURCE OF THE LUNE

Start: Newbiggin-on-Lune. Grid Ref: 706 051
Distance: 8½ miles (13½km)
OS Maps: Pathfinder 607 or Landranger 91
Walking Time: 4½ hours

Walkers exploring the Lune Valley may finally come to Newbiggin-on-Lune, where the river begins. This splendid, though fairly strenuous, walk climbs to a ridge leading to Randygill Top at an altitude 2,047 feet (624m), one of the finest viewpoints in the Howgills, before continuing its horseshoe of Weasda to the top of Green Bell – the Lune's source is 160 feet (50m) below the summit. The return is a gentle descent over Ravenstonedale Common. Although there are good tracks most of the way there are two steep climbs with tussocky grass. Newbiggin, off the A685, has space for a few cars.

Just off the main road from Tebay to Kirkby Stephen, the peaceful little village of Newbiggin lies at the foot of the northern slopes of the Howgill Fells and at the head of the lovely east-west valley of the upper Lune. This broad, glaciated valley is a truly pastoral scene, where each farm is sheltered in its own side gill and cluster of trees. The scattered nature of the communities and names like Raisgill, Ellergill, and Weasdale all point to their Viking origins, places where, a thousand years ago, Norsemen first established their flocks of sheep and herds of pigs.

If you ask the people in Newbiggin about the source of the Lune, one of the places they will direct you to is over the road to St Helens Well. This ancient spring of holy water begins next to the site of St Helens chapel – a mere grassy platform – where it flows along a flowery channel, then through the village, to join up with Bessy Beck, Drybeck and waters from another nearby spring to make the beginnings of the Lune. The main feeder, high up on the sides of Green Bell, is Greenside Beck, becoming Drybeck as it reaches limestone on the south side of the village.

Newbiggin is neat with a small green and a centre surrounded by houses and cottages. One of the houses is the former church of St Aidens, built in 1892 with a gift of £2,000

from John Fothergill of Brownber. Opposite is Bovil House which has a fortified yard. The school, too, is now a private house, the post office has gone and the last two shops have recently given up business. New enterprises include a nursery for plants, with cafe, and trout farm.

The most famous person of Newbiggin was Elizabeth Gaunt, daughter of Anthony Fothergill of Brownber. In 1685 she became the last woman to be burnt alive – at Tyburn, London. She was an anabaptist, noted for her benevolence, who concealed a rebel, who then betrayed her for a reward. The rebel was pardoned and she was burned for her charity. 'I did but relieve a poor family, and lo, I must die for it.' The burning was witnessed by William Penn (founder of Pennsylvania), who said that when she 'calmly disposed the straw about her in such a manner as to shorten her sufferings, all the bystanders burst into tears'.

The old railway station on the west side of the village used to serve Ravenstonedale, Newbiggin's parent village just over a mile away (2km), and the old line from Tebay as far as Newbiggin is now followed by the Kirkby Stephen road which bypasses the village.

From the village green, go by the side of the village hall and through the right hand of two white gates. The right of way passes

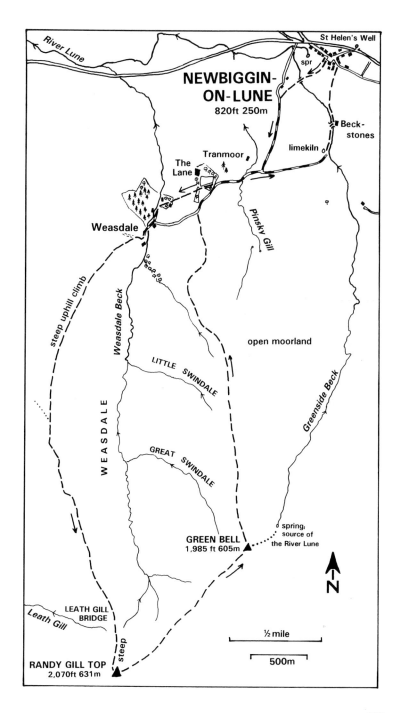

under an ancient spinning gallery which has steps up to it. Go through a door and on to a stile. Cross a plank bridge and two white-painted footbridges to reach the Weasdale road. Some of the small streams contain masses of white river crowfoot (or water buttercup), yellow monkey flower and forget-me-not.

Turn left along the unfenced road. In the spring months you are likely to be within earshot of the skylark for the whole of the walk. The skylark cannot be ignored as it warbles away for several minutes, hovering on high, before diving down, singing still until near the ground. Snipe, meadow pipit and curlew frequent the lower slopes. Randygill Top and Green Bell stand out ahead, while on the right is the pretty whitewashed farm-house of Tranmoor.

Turn right at the t-junction. At the bridge over Pinsky Gill, where tiny yellow flowers of black medick grow profusely, it is only a 150 yards (140m) upstream to an interesting outcrop of siltstones and limestones known as the Pinsky beds. They lie on Silurian slates, and for many years their age was uncertain as they themselves are overlain by conglomerates once assigned to the Devonian. Micro-fossils – known as conodonts – have now given a very early Carboniferous age (circa 355 million years) to both the Pinsky beds and the conglomerate.

Where the road turns to the left, carry straight on to enter the woodland by a gap in the wall. The way passes through the wood and a large meadow to a stile at the side of a roofless barn. Another short patch of wood-land brings you into the yard of Weasdale nurseries. Turn left up the lane, past the secluded cottages and farm of Weasdale.

Straight on, over Weasdale Beck, turn up to the right along the tarred track, then immediately strike off to the left to follow a wall up the sloping hillside. At the wall corner – the intake wall – keep on steeply up the fellside, aiming for the highest part of the

ridge. There is a good view left up the deep valley of Weasdale.

As you progress up the lower slopes and the ground ahead seems to be closer to the eye, look for some of the smaller plants in the boggy ground. Milkwort appears in shades of pink and blue, sundew is present and the small trailing stems of cranberry are to be seen on the sphagnum moss. Other plants among the coarse grasses include the starry green moss, polytrichum, as well as acid-tolerant flowers of tormentil and heath bed-straw.

Two or three small cairns guide you up onto the ridge and a tractor track. To the left is Weasdale, and the deep valley to the right is Bowderdale. Follow the double track that winds along the ridge. Across Weasdale is Green Bell, topped by a survey pillar, and you can see roughly the horseshoe route to be followed. Some gully erosion has now grassed over but there are some impressive gashes in the hillside, with Wild Boar Fell in the background. Look out for birds of prey and ravens around the higher ridges and summits.

Before reaching Randygill Top there is a drop to Leathgill Bridge, a superb saddle some 260 feet (80m) below the ridge. Al-though there is a steep descent into the valleys on each side, there is no track which uses this natural pass. A very steep scramble up through the tussocks of grass takes you to the cairn and the highest part of the walk.

From the grassy summit of Randygill Top is the finest panoramic view for miles around. Starting with the Eden Valley and the line of the Pennines including Cross Fell, there follows Wild Boar Fell, Baugh Fell, then Ingleborough and Whernside. The Howgills are spread before you and, on a clear day, the Lakeland mountains form a continuous profile from Coniston Old Man to Carrock Fell. Below and ahead is the Rawthey Valley and its tributary of Wandale.

From Randygill Top, turn left along the ridge, with a good track again, and head for

The handsome little pied flycatcher is always on the move, and you have to be quick to spot one in its acrobatic flight as it dives for flies.

the prominent triangulation pillar on Green Bell. The rounded grassy top is 1,985 feet (605 m) above sea level. The walk continues by bearing a little to the left, but if you wish to visit the source of the Lune, keep straight on, as if you were going on to Knoutberry, and descend steeply to a ruined sheepfold 160 feet (50m) below the summit. (Be sure you have enough energy to climb back up again!) The spring is just to the left of the sheepfold, where you should be able to get a drink of the purest cool water.

From the top of Green Bell there is a view of Smardale, a deep valley which is crossed by the tall columns of the disused railway viaduct; beyond lies the Eden Valley.

Head due north along a wheel track over Ravenstonedale Common on a gentle descent, keeping to the central ridge and the most worn of the wheel tracks and, when approaching an enclosed field over to the left, join a well-defined track which leads down to the road. Turn right along the road to Beckstones, a mile (1.6km) further on, where Greenside Beck becomes Dry Beck before becoming the River Lune in the village. A round limekiln stands on the left, and goldfinches may be seen in the area feeding from seedheads such as dandelion clocks. At Beckstones, cross the bridge to the right bank, and keep straight on over a small footbridge and field path back to Newbiggin-on-Lune.

SELECTED READING

General:

Anon, *Sedbergh, Garsdale and Dent in the Yorkshire Dales National Park* (Sedbergh Council, 1962). A guide to the area including some natural history and suggested walks.

Jessica Lofthouse, *Countrygoer's North* (Hale, 1965). Good, mainly historical background to the area.

Stan & Freda Trott, *Return to the Lune* (Douglas & Son, 1972 and 1984). A guide for the tourist.

Geology and Scenery:

Tony Waltham, *Yorkshire Dales: limestone country* (Constable, 1987). Gives details of Ease Gill and its caverns.

W Edwards and F M Trotter, *The Pennines and Adjacent Areas* (HMSO). A regional geology which includes details of the Howgills area.

History:

John Banks, *The Silent Stream* (Penwork, Leeds, 1991). A personal history of Grisedale, subtitled 'The Little Quaker Dale'.

David Boulton, *Discovering Dent and Lower Dentdale* and *Discovering Upper Dentdale* (Author, 1985). Small historical guides to old farms, meeting houses and mill sites.

Barry Cockroft, *The Dale that Died* (Dent & Sons, 1975). About the people of Grisedale over the last 100 years.

Michael Ffinch, *The Howgills and the Upper Eden Valley* (Hale, 1982). A well-written history that covers the whole area as well as the upper Eden.

Marie Hartley and Joan Ingilby, *The Old Hand-Knitters of the Dales*. Includes a chapter on the 'Terrible Knitters e' Dent'.

Dawn Robertson and Peter Koronka, *Secrets and Legends of Old Westmorland* (Pagan Press and Cumbria County Council, 1992). Tells many forgotten stories.

Adam Sedgwick, *Adam Sedgwick's Dent* (Hollett and Boulton, Dent, 1984). A reprint of two classics of dales history.

Colin Speakman, *Adam Sedgwick, Geologist and Dalesman* (Broad Oak Press and others, 1982). Standard biography of Dent's famous inhabitant.

Harry Speight, *The Craven and North West Yorkshire Highlands* (Elliot Stock, 1892. Reprint Smith Settle, 1989). A factual, historical view of the area.

Freda Trott, *Sedbergh* (Douglas & Son, Sedbergh, 1991). A recent booklet about the history of Sedbergh and district.

H A L Rice, *Kirkby Lonsdale and its Neighbourhood* (Westmorland Gazette, 1983). Local history by a former resident.

Railways:

David Joy, *Main Line Over Shap* (Dalesman, 1967). The story of the Lancaster-Carlisle railway.

W R Mitchell and David Joy, *Settle to Carlisle* (Dalesman, 1989). The story of this historic railway line over the Pennines.

Natural History:

Cumbria Naturalists Union, *Birds of Cumbria, 1991*. A useful list of species with notes about each and several distribution maps of the county.

J Ferguson-Lees (*et al*), *The Shell Guide to the Birds of Britain and Ireland*. (Michael Joseph, 1983) One of the best general bird books.

Franklyn Perring, *RSNC Guide to British Wild Flowers* (Country Life Books, 1984). Very useful for learning common species and sorting out 'look-alikes'.

Walking:

A. Wainwright, *Walks on the Howgill Fells, A Coast to Coast Walk* and *Walks in Limestone Country* (Westmorland Gazette, various editions).

Fiction:

Mary Howett, *Hope On, Hope Ever!* (1840; new edition 1988, Dales Historical Monographs, Dent) A story set in Dentdale.

INDEX